Praise for
COMPELLING FORCE LEADERSHIP

John Robison lives out what he writes in *Compelling Force Leadership*. He is an example of what true servant leadership should look like. John's humility (thinking of others before himself) permeates throughout the pages of this book. I'm grateful for the profound, transformative impact of this well-written resource!
—**Blaine Boyer, Former MLB pitcher and current Kansas City Royals Special Assistant Dedicated to Leadership Development**

I thoroughly enjoyed this book . . . Reading and learning from other people's experiences is one of my favorite pastimes. John's approach to writing this book, much like his approach to being our Director of Public Safety, comes from a place of honesty and humility. He does not take credit where credit is not due, and he does not pretend to be someone he is not. That is a rare trait for someone who is the leader of 250 hard, charging police and firemen in our city. It would be very easy in such an adrenaline-intensive environment to let that go to your head . . . But that's not John. Make sure you read and reread the part about the power of the word . . . That was one of my favorite lessons!
—**Brian Will, Serial Entrepreneur, WSJ Best Selling Author City Council in Alpharetta, Georgia**

Compelling Force Leadership is a very relatable yet impactful leadership volume. Robison employs an effective structure, one that emphasizes what he calls "the 3Ps of leadership": people, purpose, and passion. The book is written in a very honest and personable tone that makes for an easy read. In addition to providing important conceptual food for thought, Robison concludes each significant takeaway with a section termed "Practical

Points." *Compelling Force Leadership* provides hands-on material for the reader. Law enforcement professionals will gain much from reading this book!

—Dr. Dean Dabney, Professor and Chair of Criminal Justice & Criminology at Georgia State University and Executive Director of the Leadership Development Institute of Georgia

Every leader has a choice in their own personal leadership: Am I going to be transactional (for me) or transformational (for others)? In this amazing book, my good friend Chief John Robison breaks down how to be a transformational leader in the selfish culture we have to lead! I love this book not only for the great information and application, but also because Chief Robison is a transformational leader himself! Great read!!!

—Mike Linch, Senior Pastor at NorthStar Church and host of the *Linch with a Leader* podcast

COMPELLING FORCE

LEADERSHIP

COMPELLING
FORCE→
LEADERSHIP

How Leaders Can Use
Their Influence to Effectively
Lead People with Purpose and Passion

———

JOHN ROBISON

B

BOOKLOGIX
Alpharetta, Georgia

This publication is meant as a source of valuable information for the reader, however it is not meant as a substitute for direct expert assistance. If such level of assistance is required, the services of a competent professional should be sought.

ISBN: 978-1-6653-0568-6 - Paperback
eISBN: 978-1-6653-0569-3 - eBook

These ISBNs are the property of BookLogix for the express purpose of sales and distribution of this title. The content of this book is the property of the copyright holder only. BookLogix does not hold any ownership of the content of this book and is not liable in any way for the materials contained within. The views and opinions expressed in this book are the property of the Author/Copyright holder, and do not necessarily reflect those of BookLogix.

Library of Congress Control Number: 2023908621

⊗This paper meets the requirements of ANSI/NISO Z39.48-1992
(Permanence of Paper)

Author photo taken by Katherine Fies.

060123

To all the men and women that serve in public safety.
You are the consummate public servants, and I greatly
appreciate the sacrifices you and your families
make while protecting and serving our communities.

Definition of Influence: The capacity or power of persons or things to be a COMPELLING FORCE on or produce effects on the actions, behavior, opinions, etc. of OTHERS.
—Dictionary.com

CONTENTS

Introduction   xiii

PART ONE: A Compelling Leader
Chapter 1: A Boss vs. A Leader   3
Chapter 2: Leadership That Transforms   11

PART TWO: 3P Leadership—
                Adding Value to People
Chapter 3: It's All about Perspective   25
Chapter 4: Everything Starts
                with Engagement   31
Chapter 5: Critical Communication   45
Chapter 6: Critical Communication—
                Practical Points   59
Chapter 7: An Ongoing Development   73

PART THREE: 3P Leadership—Purpose
Chapter 8: Purpose-Driven Leadership   89
Chapter 9: Purpose for Your People   97
Chapter 10: Promoting Your Purpose   115

PART FOUR: 3P Leadership—Passion
Chapter 11: A Penchant for Passion   133
Chapter 12: Keeping the Saw Sharp   153
Chapter 13: Keep On Growing   165
Chapter 14: Conclusion   177

Acknowledgments   183

INTRODUCTION

I LOVED BEING a detective. Of all the positions I have held in law enforcement, being Detective Robison has always been my favorite. Looking back, I am not even sure I was that good at it, but I loved immersing myself in the investigative process. There was a great deal of satisfaction associated with being able to bring a case to fruition. As a detective that was often assigned child cases, I especially enjoyed locking up people that harmed children. As far as I was concerned, I had found my niche and wanted to spend the rest of my career being Detective Robison.

All of this changed when my chief called me into his office to tell me I was next on the promotional list, and he needed me to go back to the road as a front-line supervisor. That year, I had done what "I was supposed to do" by going through the promotional process. Honestly, I never really imagined there would be any chance of getting promoted, and I was just fine with that. However, I was suddenly torn between staying where I was or accepting a promotion to a position I was not overly excited about taking. After seeking some wise counsel and realizing it could be a career-limiting move to turn down a promotion, I was once again in a patrol car supervising a uniform shift.

Like many of you reading this can appreciate, I quickly found myself in charge with absolutely no clue what I was doing. I looked at some of the great officers I was now supervising, thinking I had no business telling them what to do. I had no awareness of the differences between having rank and being a leader. Ultimately, I did not feel I had the credibility to lead, and I was not sure how to change that.

So, I did the best I could and focused on trying to take care of my officers. I had been fortunate enough to work for some supervisors that took good care of me, and I figured it made sense to try to do the same in my new position. It was here that I began a new chapter in my career.

And . . . it was here that I truly fell in love with leadership.

Over a decade later, I have come to appreciate the privilege and responsibility of leading others, especially those that have chosen a career that exists to serve people. In a nutshell, I have learned leadership is all about people, and those people are most effectively led by leaders that lead with purpose and passion.

That's it . . . leadership is ultimately about adding value to people by leading with purpose and passion.

This 3P Leadership (adding value to *p*eople by leading with *p*urpose and *p*assion) approach is the foundation of this book. An effective leader is a leader that is always growing. The following pages of this book will cover several leadership topics that will hopefully benefit us all as we continue to grow and develop, no matter where you are on the leadership spectrum.

Maybe you are currently in a leadership role for the first time or have simply found an interest in the topic of leadership. Or you could be in a middle management position, navigating through the intricacies of leading others while being led yourself. Some of you may be reading this as a grizzly veteran of leadership—and possibly asking, "Why am I considering reading a book on leadership from this guy?" Whatever stage of leadership you are in, my hope is that you discover what I have found when exploring this topic: The more I read about it, study it, and hear from other people doing it, the more I will grow as a leader. Heck, you may not agree with some of the book's content. Nevertheless, if it gets those mental gears moving, and at least causes you to examine where you are as a leader and what you can do to more effectively add value to people through leading with purpose and passion, then I will consider it mission accomplished.

As we get ready to dive into talking about the most important part of leadership—the people—I want to be transparent and upfront about myself so it's clear where I'm coming from when writing this book.

- **I can't take much credit:** I am often asked by "aspiring" leaders what I did to get where I am. Well, I would love to be able to tell you I had a great game plan, and I was very strategic and intentional in getting to a place where I lead an organization of 250 of the greatest people on the face of the planet. However, any such claim would simply not be true. Honestly, one of the main reasons why I am here is because this is where God has taken me. I am a man of faith that strives (not always effectively) to fulfill God's purpose for my life. Also, I have been very fortunate to have some great people invest in me and create opportunities for me to develop and be successful. I owe a great deal of gratitude to a lot of people. Most effective leaders can point to specific people in their life that played a huge role in getting them to where they are in their careers.
- **I'm not always successful at accomplishing the things I discuss in this book:** I am truly a believer in centering leadership around people, being a mission-minded leader, and leading with a passion and zeal that keeps me sharp and on point. I am thoroughly convinced this is the most effective way to lead, regardless of who you are or where you are leading. I often fall flat on my face when it comes to consistently executing these leadership principles. I've read a lot of leadership books by really good authors that come across as being somewhat flawless in their execution of leadership. That is by no means a knock against those authors. However, if that is what you are looking for here, you have grabbed the wrong book. Much of my growth has

come through screwing up, and I still have a lot more screwing up—I mean growing—to do. A perfect example of this is communication. One of the biggest struggles of leadership in any organization is effective communication up and down the chain. I talk about communication in this book. I can preach to you the importance of communication as it relates to a healthy culture and making your people feel valued. I can give you several practical tools I have used to ensure quality communication is more consistent where you lead. Yet, there are times I continue to struggle in this area. Just when I think we are starting to get it right, I am often made painfully aware of how much more work we need to do to get better at effectively communicating. The struggle for effective communication is never-ending. If you feel like you know what you should do, but sometimes mess up in actually doing it, this is the right book for you.

- **Much of what I have learned, and even share in this book, I have learned from others:** From early elementary school through the first years of graduate school, I absolutely hated reading. I would get bored and distracted within five minutes of picking up a book. However, when I started learning to love leadership, I also started learning to love reading. Now, I cannot read enough. General Mattis once wrote; "If you have not read hundreds of books, you are functionally illiterate, and you will be incompetent because your personal experiences alone aren't broad enough to sustain you." Now, I feel that might be a tad over the top. I don't know if I would call someone who hasn't read hundreds of books illiterate, but I do agree with his overall premise. We are very much limiting ourselves as leaders, and in life in general, if we don't read about other people's personal experiences. I can attest to this. Much of my growth as a leader has come from reading books by other effective leaders.

There are two other groups of people that have helped add to my leadership knowledge. When I first became a police chief, I was so blessed to be in an area that was full of experienced, quality police chiefs that were willing to pour into me throughout the years. I would meet them for lunch, call them with questions and seek their counsel. Part of becoming a good leader is hanging out with other good leaders!

I have also gained a tremendous amount of insight from public safety personnel all over the country. I am fortunate to be able to teach leadership classes for a national law enforcement training company, and I typically travel one or two times a month to talk to police officers, dispatchers, firefighters, and civilian personnel about leadership. Often, these classes are also full of people in leadership positions. I cannot tell you how much I have gained from meeting so many great people in our profession that truly want to serve their departments and their communities. I often hear their frustrations about the leadership deficiencies in their departments, as well as hear some really good ideas on effective leadership approaches that are being implemented where they work. So, I hear a lot of the good and the bad of leadership, which has certainly impacted my growth as a leader.

MY LEADERSHIP PERSPECTIVE

My current, "official" title is Director of Public Safety, but the people in our department simply refer to me as Chief, which I prefer. I started my career as a police officer in late 2001, but my current role has me leading police, fire, and 911. I have been serving in this position since January 2017. Before that, I served as a Police Chief in another metro-Atlanta city. Our department is made up of the most selfless public servants you will find anywhere in our great land. Our team has the privilege of serving a progressive, vibrant city in the metro-Atlanta area. I must tell you, I am blessed with a fantastic job, serving in a wonderful area.

Obviously, a great deal of my leadership perspective is based on my experience in Public Safety. A lot of the examples and stories I provide will reflect my experiences in this profession. I truly hope all readers will discover what I found to be true years ago. The tenets of effective leadership are applicable in all areas, regardless of the profession. Whether you are a middle manager of a small business, a CEO of a large corporation, or a volunteer leader in a non-profit organization, the most effective leadership principles are universal. One of my favorite leadership authors, Jocko Willink, is a great example of this. If you don't know who he is, look him up and take the time to read his first book, *Extreme Ownership*. Jocko was a Navy Seal commander with an amazing military career. One of the attributes that makes him such an effective author is when he writes on leadership or discusses it on his podcasts, his content can be applied to any leadership role in any profession.

MY REASON FOR WRITING THIS BOOK

One of the police majors in my department once described leadership as "emotional labor." I have never forgotten that . . . because it's so true. Leadership is hard. Actually, trying to be an effective, transformational leader is hard. Sometimes I joke with our staff that it would be much easier to stay in my office and be an autocratic leader that just tells people what to do. Yet, I know in my heart this is not the kind of leadership our people deserve or need. Being a Chief has been the best and most difficult job I have ever had. My job is not dangerous, like the jobs our police officers and firefighters do every day. They truly have the toughest jobs, and that is one of the many reasons why I need to do my best to be sure they feel like they matter, because they do.

However, being a leader is difficult in so many other ways. Trying to create/maintain a healthy culture, managing a group of very diverse personalities, and striving to effectively serve our wonderful citizens while also serving our city leadership is a never-ending mental and emotional roller coaster ride. You may be serving customers instead of citizens and serving a board instead of city officials, but if you are in leadership, you know the roller coaster ride I am talking about. When I hear or read about the struggles of other leaders—when I come across great leadership strategies or practical ideas, when I hear or read the circumstances other leaders face and think "I know exactly what that is like!"—it helps me. It helps me be a more effective leader. It helps re-energize me. It helps me remember why I do this. My desire is that you get a little of all that when you read this book, and it helps you become a better leader.

PART ONE

A COMPELLING LEADER

"Certain circumstances call for leaders to perform like a boss for the good of the organization."

Chapter 1

A BOSS VS. A LEADER

I WAS BORN in 1971. In 1973, a show was introduced on television called *The Six Million Dollar Man*. There were ninety-nine episodes and six made-for-TV movies about astronaut Steve Austin (also known as the Bionic Man), who was severely injured when his spaceship crashed, and he was basically turned into a cyborg after the government rebuilt him with machine parts. I started watching the show when I was around six, and during that time, there was no greater American hero than the six-million-dollar man. In 1984, another show was introduced that greatly impacted millions of American teenagers called *Miami Vice*. Detective Sonny Crocket and Ricardo Tubbs were the coolest dressed detectives in the history of all law enforcement shows. I must confess, when I was in high school, there were some wardrobe decisions made based on what these guys were wearing while catching bad guys.

So, as a kid/teenager growing up watching these shows, you can imagine how thrilled I was to be able to have a part in a movie starring Lee Majors (Steve Austin) and Phillip Michael Thomas (Ricardo Tubbs). That's right . . . I had the chance to be in a movie with the Bionic Man and Detective Tubbs! This movie was being filmed in the city where I worked in 2003. They needed some extras for police-related scenes (including a scene where the entire SWAT team gets taken out), and they also needed an officer to say, "How's it going, Jimmy?" to the main character, played by Lee Majors. Clearly, word had gotten out about my acting prowess, and I was given the part of the officer that got out of his patrol car at headquarters, along with another officer, and was directed to inquire how Jimmy was doing as he walked past me.

For you *Seinfeld* fans, it was kind of like the episode where Kramer was tasked with saying; "These pretzels are making me thirsty" for a Woody Allen movie. I remember having a conversation with the director, who told me all about how the premier would take place at the Fox Theater in Atlanta, and I could bring my wife to this Hollywood-like event where the movie *"Fate"* would become a box office smash. And who knew . . . it could've been the beginning of a whole new career in acting for this patrol officer. Heck, it could've been a great movie in itself. . . . Patrol officer putting his life on the line every day gets discovered by Hollywood in a small role with his childhood heroes? That's got "movie based on a true story" written all over it!

Well, *"Fate"* was a complete bomb that went straight to DVD. It never made it to the theaters, and there was never a movie premiere at the Fox Theater. That movie, and my future acting career, both went down in flames. However, to this day, I can say I had a line in a movie with two television icons (okay . . . former icons). Now, does that mean I can call myself an actor? I filled a role in a movie, so that means I am an actor, correct? Of course not. Me being in a movie does not qualify me to be an actor. Being a good actor takes a lot of work, training, preparation, and skill. Just because I was given an opportunity to briefly "act" does not make me an actor.

The same can be said for people that fill recognized leadership roles in organizations. Just because a person's title supposedly correlates with leadership does not automatically equate to that person being a leader. Using the term "rank" from my profession . . . there can be people without rank that are leaders, and there are people with rank that are not leaders. Title and authority do not automatically equate to leadership.

We have all been given directives. To put it simply, we have been told what to do numerous times. In the early stages of our lives, we were often given orders by adults. Our parents, our teachers, our coaches, etc., all gave us commands without much concern about our opinions or concerns regarding those commands. How many times did we get the response "because I said so" when questioning a directive given by our parents? I remember getting frustrated because I wanted to know why. Why would they deny my requests, or why would they insist that I comply with their demands? Yet, I found myself providing the same response when I became a dad. Sometimes, it was just easier to utilize my "authority" as a father, versus trying to provide an adequate explanation when being asked "why" over and over again by my children.

It's one thing to pull the "authority" card as a father. I now understand that my parents usually knew what was best, and I often did not have the ability to completely grasp why their directives were appropriate for the situation, and often for me. However, people that rely on their authority to get people to carry out their duties on the job are not practicing effective leadership. It's imperative to understand that authority does not equate to leadership and being a leader does not require having recognized authority.

In my world of public safety, rank is considered a cornerstone of leadership. Police and fire especially operate on a paramilitary foundation, with rank and chain of command being at the heart of all operations. Don't get me wrong, rank and chain of command are important and have their place in the military and in public safety. Yet, when men and women *rely* on that rank to get people to fulfill their duties, they are not being leaders, they are being bosses. I can recall police supervisors pointing to their collar brass and telling people when asked why, "because I said so." That's not leadership, that's being a boss.

The same goes for other organizations. There are people that are given recognized authority to operate in supervisory/management roles. Those roles are vitally important to the success of those organizations. But it's not the authority that makes them leaders, it is their ability to *influence.* Leadership is not about authority, it's all about influence. Some of the most effective leaders I have seen and worked with were not in positions of authority. They had earned their leadership roles in the department by garnering influence with their coworkers.

Please don't miss an important point. There are times when you need someone with authority to take the lead in providing decisive direction. This is especially true in my profession. If we have a major structure fire, an incident where SWAT has been called in, etc., we must have someone utilize their recognized authority and take command. At that point, their job is to give clear direction and tell people what to do. There are times in my role as Chief when I have to give clear orders and make decisions with little or no input from others. Certain circumstances call for leaders to perform like a boss for the good of the organization.

For example, executing discipline is very much a boss-like function. I am doing what's best for the organization when I consistently hold people accountable, and that can result in engaging in direct actions that are necessary and sometimes unpleasant. I have terminated police officers, firefighters, and dispatchers. I have demoted and suspended employees. It's one of the tough parts of the job, but it is very much a part of what I must do as a leader in my organization. Most of what we discuss in this book relates to the importance of establishing and maintaining a compelling force, influence-based leadership perspective. I do however want to be clear that I am fully aware of the moments we have to be autocratic and direct in our roles. These scenarios do not typically apply to the day-to-day operations of leading a team, unit, division, or organization. I have found these times are somewhat rare, and the most effective leadership approach is centered around what we focus on throughout this book.

I don't generally get excited about definitions, but I love dictionary.com's definition of influence:

The capacity or power of persons or things to be a COMPELLING FORCE on or produce effects on the actions, behavior, opinions, etc. of OTHERS.

A compelling force! What a clear nexus between leadership and influence this provides us. Men and women that have influence can greatly affect people's actions, behaviors, and opinions. Is that not at the heart of what we are supposed to do as leaders? We want to influence our people in a manner that helps foster behaviors that result in achieving the mission of our organizations (see Part 3). Can employees without rank or authority be a compelling force in their organization? Absolutely! One of the most used phrases in our department is "make it better." It's literally printed in large letters on one of our walls on the first floor of our headquarters. The idea is we are always striving to make our agency better. Although there are several areas our agency excels in, we should never stop trying to "make it better." Do you know which employees typically raise our overall level of performance as a team? The people that intentionally use their influence and proactively work to make sure we are always improving and working toward fulfilling our mission. Those employees are a compelling force!

One of the greatest leadership books written in my generation is *The 7 Habits of Highly Successful People* by Steven Covey. This is a must-read for anyone striving to be an effective leader. He discusses in great detail the role of influence in organizations. I really cannot do justice to the brilliance of his writing, but he does a great job of describing our "circle of concern" and our "circle of influence." Unfortunately, most of the items in our circle of concern are items or issues we simply have little or no control over. Conversely, our circle of control—usually a much smaller circle—are things we *have the ability to change.*

Good leaders focus their energy on issues, problems, concerns, etc. they can change for the better. They value opportunities to act as a compelling force for positive change, and they use their influence to make that happen. The really cool part about this approach to leadership is they are not only making it better, they are expanding the third circle—the leader's circle of influence—which will give them more opportunities to make it better!

In the next chapter, I am going to discuss a style of leadership that focuses on the importance of developing a healthy culture by adding value to our people. This leadership style is reliant upon leaders utilizing their influence. As stated throughout this chapter, that leadership is not contingent upon recognized authority. Power and authority can be used to get enough done to keep the doors open and the lights on. However, when people rely less on rank/position and more on influence and adding value to people, the results will far exceed the authority-based leadership approach. Research absolutely supports this concept. At the end of the day, *leading* is not about power, it's about *influence.*

An officer that worked for me got promoted and struggled with the "respect my authority" syndrome early on in his new role. To protect the innocent, I will refer to him as "Captain Davis." I promise I have never had a Captain Davis work for me, so I am not calling anyone out here. Also, let me say this guy was a great guy who had a lot of talent. His heart was in the right place, but he fell into the power trap that comes with a leadership position like so many have at one time or another.

One day, we were visiting a local high school in our jurisdiction. As was usually the case, when I met people for the first time, I simply introduced myself as John. On the other hand, Captain Davis had a little bit of a different approach as he would make sure people were aware of his rank when he introduced himself each time as CAPTAIN Davis. Imagine each of his introductions being presented in a very official, loud, and stern voice. Later that day, after we left, I tried to help him see the people we met could care less about our rank. Sure, a few former members of the military and a limited amount of people that understand law enforcement may have grasped the "importance" of his title, but for the most part, nobody was impressed or cared. The big-picture point I was trying to help him grasp was not to make his job or role about his rank. I encouraged him to be the man I knew him to be, and when people saw who he genuinely was as a law enforcement officer and man, his leadership qualities would be evident. I wanted him to see it was not about him being CAPTAIN Davis, it was about the influence he exerts in our department and community.

By the way, we no longer work together, but he continues to have a very successful career in law enforcement.

PRACTICAL POINTS

What is your process for promoting people into recognized leadership roles? In the world of public safety, we often rank candidates based on a written test, interview panel, in-box exercises, etc. It's not uncommon for points to also be given to candidates based on their resumes as well. Candidates get scored and ranked, and whoever is on the top of the list often gets promoted next.

Is this really the most effective way to ensure the right people are getting promoted? Regardless of what the process is, the goal should always be to promote people that are already demonstrating the leadership qualities that matter to the organization. We should not promote people that are simply good at their job and then hope they turn into good leaders. We should promote people that have already demonstrated their influence in the organization and have shown what it means to "make it better."

We have our supervisors complete questionnaires for each candidate. I have found that their input is crucial, as they work with the candidates regularly, and they can provide a lot of insight into who most likely will fit what we are looking for in a leadership role. Once all of their input is gathered, our command staff meets to go over the feedback and determine who the best candidate for promotion is at that time. A formal recommendation of candidates for promotion is presented to me, and I almost always accept the team's choice for the best candidates to promote.

No process is perfect and free from subjectivity, but I will say that overall, this process has resulted in the promotion of the right people helping us create a healthy culture and successful organization.

Chapter 2

LEADERSHIP THAT TRANSFORMS

IT WAS SOMETIME in 2011, and I was just assigned to Lieutenant over Support Services, which included the Office of Professional Standards (OPS). One of the important functions of OPS was to oversee the hiring of new officers. The process for hiring back then was similar to what most departments do today:

- Job announcement
- Physical agility test
- Written test
- Panel interview
- Psychological evaluation
- Background investigation (including taking a polygraph)
- Interview with the Chief
- Hired

For the first process I supervised, we had four open positions we needed to fill. We announced the opening and set a date for the physical agility test on an upcoming Saturday morning. One hundred and sixty people showed up to compete for four openings. One hundred and sixty! Of course, there were several that did not pass the physical agility test. For those that did pass, I then met with them and provided a list of disqualifiers that would immediately remove them from consideration. Examples of disqualifiers included a DUI in the last seven years, any previous use of a felony-level drug, or marijuana use in the last three years, just to name a few. Several people got up and left, including one guy that smoked dope that morning on the way to our testing!

Now we were down to approximately one hundred applicants. Those applicants then took a written exam. About twenty failed, leaving eighty eligible applicants. Once the rest of the steps were completed, we ended up with approximately fifty applicants that were eligible for hire. Not only did we fill those four positions quickly, but we also had a list of applicants that we could choose from until we tested again the next year. This hiring stuff was pretty easy . . .

Those days are long gone.

We now have *weekly* testings. Each week, we normally have five to ten candidates scheduled to come and test for police officer positions. Typically, about half of those scheduled to attend actually show up and take the test. We have been fortunate to hire some excellent candidates, but it is more difficult than ever to hire and retain good public safety personnel. People are leaving the profession in droves for safer jobs, better hours, higher pay, and more stable family lives.

This problem does not just exist in public safety. During the last year, we have often heard the phrase "the great resignation" describe the mass exodus taking place in America's workforce. Ever since the dreaded Covid-19 came on the scene, we have had a mass reduction in our country's workforce. According to the Society for Human Resource Management, in 2021, 47.8 million workers quit their jobs. This averages out to nearly 4 million each month, which makes 2021 the highest average on record, surpassing the 2019 average of 3.5 million.[1]

---

[1] Shrm, "Interactive Chart: How Historic Has the Great Resignation Been?," SHRM (SHRM, April 20, 2022), https://www.shrm.org/resourcesandtools/hr-topics/talent-acquisition/pages/interactive-quits-level-by-year.aspx.

On a recent Sunday, my wife, daughter, and I went to a local restaurant after church. They, like so many other restaurants we go to, had a sign in the window stating; NOW HIRING SERVERS. Once seated, we watched two young servers work their tails off trying to handle the crowd. This is now a common scene throughout our country, especially in service-oriented occupations. It's representative of a huge challenge for all types of businesses and corporations. That challenge is not only finding good, qualified people to hire, but keeping them once they are on the job.

The title of this book gives what I call the three important Ps of leadership: Adding value to *people* by leading with *purpose* and *passion*. Throughout the rest of this book, this concept will be described as 3P leadership. Now more than ever, the first *P* in 3P, people, must be the primary focus of leadership. Part 2 focuses on the importance of making leadership all about the people we lead.

Our best shot at finding and retaining good people is to create a culture where leadership adds value to our people. I firmly believe that now more than ever, we need leaders that are engaged in a transformational leadership approach. Copious amounts of research have demonstrated this leadership style will most likely result in a higher level of employee-job satisfaction and organizational commitment. These leaders are perceived as more approachable and more responsive to employee needs, which creates a higher level of job commitment. Transformational leadership is ultimately about creating a healthy culture and adding value to our personnel.

Back in the 1970s, A researcher named James MacGregor Burns created a new paradigm in leadership, breaking down leadership into two distinct concepts: transactional and transformational. In his book, *Leadership* (1978), Burns asserted that transactional leaders lead through the use of social exchange. A great example of this assertion is one many of you can probably relate to from personal experience. When I was growing up, I was completely unaware my dad was being a "transactional" father when he gave me a list of chores to do. If I did those chores in a timely manner, I received an allowance. I met the expectation, and I was given something in return.

Politicians often find themselves in transactional relationships. A constituent or lobbyist provides something a politician needs, and that politician somehow returns the favor (always on the up and up of course). In our world of public safety, transactional leadership is common, especially since we operate so similarly to the military, which has almost always ascribed to a transactional style of leadership. Some transaction examples:

- Do your job = Get paid and keep your job
- Do more than is expected of you = Get a raise
- Be really good at your job = Get promoted
- Handle a specific project well = Get a bonus

Transformational leaders, on the other hand, differ from transactional leaders in that they strive to inspire followers to excel in their roles. They use various strategies and tools to motivate their followers to achieve much in their jobs. Can that great work be rewarded (transactional)? Of course. Nonetheless, that's not the driving force behind the employee's high level of quality of work. Transformational leaders desire to add value to the men and women on their team. They want to invest in them, develop them, and help them achieve success. The needs of followers are focused on by the leader, as well as empowering them to align their work with the organization's mission, vision, and goals. This empowerment will create a high level of buy-in by the employee. Transformational leaders effectively demonstrate to employees their value and how their positions correlate with meeting the mission of the organization.[2]

When these two types of approaches were originally researched, they were viewed as leadership styles that could not

---

[2] Bernard M. Bass and Ronald E. Riggio, *Transformational Leadership,* Second Edition (New York: Psychology Press, 2006).

coexist. Basically, leaders implemented one or the other. There was no room for overlap between the two. For example, as a chief, I theoretically cannot focus on investing in and developing our men and women *and* implement a system where employees do their job well and receive a benefit in return. To use a more specific example, Burns would say it's not possible for me to focus on inspiring and motivating employees to grow and be more innovative (transformational) and have a system in place where employees must meet specific criteria to earn the opportunity to get promoted (transactional).

Another researcher named Bernard Bass showed that both styles can coexist. He came after Burns and looked at transactional versus transformational leadership, especially in the military, business, and educational organizations. Bass's research is now considered the foundation of transformational leadership theory. His research demonstrated transformational leadership was a more effective approach than the transactional approach due to how it inspired followers to exceed expectations. He believed inspiring employees through adding value to them ultimately increased their level of commitment to their organizations while helping to create future leaders.[3] Basically, it's leaders creating and developing future leaders. Bass felt both styles could coexist and be successful in ensuring an organization's goals and objectives are achieved. Ultimately, leaders that were transformational and also integrated some transactional elements would achieve much more than a leader that only implemented a transactional style of leadership.[4]

Transformational leaders will typically emphasize the tenets

---

[3] Stewart, Jan. "Transformational Leadership: An Evolving Concept Examined through the Works of Burns, Bass, Avolio, and Leithwood." *Canadian Journal of Educational Administration and Policy.* 2006. https://files.eric.ed.gov/fulltext/EJ843441.pdf.

[4] Lowe, Kevin B., K.Galen Kroeck, and Nagaraj Sivasubramaniam. "Effectiveness Correlates of Transformational and Transactional Leadership: A Meta-Analytic Review of the MLQ Literature." The Leadership Quarterly. JAI, 1996. https://www.sciencedirect.com/science/article/pii/S1048984396900272.

of transformational leadership as they inspire and motivate others. Also, there is often a place for that transformational approach to be integrated with some basic transactional tenets. For example, imagine a manager that leads a team that is considered the highest functioning team in the organization. Employees work hard to earn the opportunity to be a part of this team. In this scenario, the manager has just received a clear directive from the CEO on new goals that must be achieved by end of the year. The manager meets with his team and communicates to them their new roles and schedules and makes it clear that if they want to continue to be a part of this highly sought-after team, they will follow his plan in order to achieve the new goals. This is a clear example of transactional leadership. Do what you are told and in return you get to stay on the team.

Now, imagine that same scenario with a transformational leader. He meets with his team to explain the new expectations and goals that must be achieved. He challenges the team to work together to determine the best plan to ensure these goals are met and then present to him their ideas. The manager clearly values their input, and knows that as a group working together, there is a greater likelihood of employee buy-in and success. The manager is being transformational in his approach. The team understands that they must meet the new goals in order to ensure they have the opportunity to continue to be a part of this elite team. That part is still transactional in nature, but the leader is ultimately acting as a transformational leader.

I love the definition Bass created for transformational leadership:

> Authentic transformational leaders motivate followers to work for transcendental goals that go beyond immediate self-interest. What is right and good to do becomes important. Transformational leaders move followers to transcend their own self-interest for the good of the group, organization, or country. Transformational leaders motivate followers and other

constituencies to do more than they originally expected to do as they strive to higher-order outcomes.[5]

Transformational leadership has now emerged as one of the most researched leadership theories.[6] Why? Because it's what people desire, and it leads to higher levels of employee job satisfaction and a stronger commitment to their organization. Conversely, those that work for transactional leaders have a lower level of job satisfaction and organizational commitment.[7] People desire to be led by leaders that invest in them, care about them, and help them improve. When people work in a culture founded upon transformational principles, they are more inclined to excel as employees. Good for them. Good for the team. Good for those being served. We all have needs, and transformational leaders can not only identify those needs but can also respond to them.[8] When leaders focus on identifying and responding to employee needs, this results in a highly effective combination of greater employee satisfaction and a better quality of work being provided.

There are four specific aspects of transformational leadership that help create a culture where job satisfaction and employee commitment is evident: idealized influence, inspirational motivation, intellectual stimulation, and individualized consideration.[9] When each of these tenets of leadership are exhibited by a transformational leader, a foundation is created for the development and sustainment of a healthy culture. Consider this . . . if you run a business that services customers in some capacity and

[5] Bass and Riggio, pp. 133.

[6] Caillier, James Gerard. "Apa PsycNet." American Psychological Association. American Psychological Association. Accessed February 14, 2023. https://psycnet.apa.org/record/2014-16925-003.

[7] Hater, John J., and Bernard M. Bass. "Apa PsycNet." American Psychological Association. American Psychological Association, 1988. https://psycnet.apa.org/record/1989-13808-001.

[8] Bass and Riggio.

[9] Bass, Bernard M., and Bruce J. Avolio. "Transformational Leadership and Organizational Culture." JSTOR, 1993. https://www.jstor.org/stable/40862298.

your employees have a high level of job satisfaction, then they are much more likely to provide quality work. As this occurs, there is an increased likelihood of the customer being satisfied with the service he or she received from your company. When your customers are satisfied with the service your people provide, you are more apt to run a successful business.

You are satisfied, your employees are satisfied, and your customers are satisfied. I guess it is actually a win-win-win! Let's take a look at the four aspects of transformational leadership.

IDEALIZED INFLUENCE

There's that word again—influence. This aspect of leadership relates to a person's ability to provide a role model for followers. They are a compelling force through role modeling what matters. People in the organization can look to their leadership and see the mission and values of the organization on display. Transformational leaders are focused on their people. Therefore, they provide a consistent example of centering their roles around taking care of their employees and those they serve in their business. Transformational leaders don't just preach putting others first, they demonstrate this behavior consistently. If we want to be a compelling influence, we must demonstrate through our actions what we value most. Leaders that don't practice what they preach, which unfortunately is not uncommon, will never gain the trust and credibility they need to effectively lead their people through being influential.

INSPIRATIONAL MOTIVATION

This concept is connected to a leader's ability to motivate and inspire those they lead. They are effective at communicating the mission and vision of the organization, and followers have a clear understanding of their leader's expectations. We will dig much deeper into this topic in chapters 7 and 8, but effective leaders motivate their people to provide a quality work product through creating purpose. We all have expectations. The problem is we don't always do an adequate job of ensuring our people know and understand our expectations. Some of the most effective CEOs in our world today are not only visionary leaders but have the ability to inspire their followers to buy into that same vision they so strongly believe in and value.

INTELLECTUAL STIMULATION

This aspect is one of my personal favorites and refers to a leader's encouragement to employ others to engage in creativity and innovation. It's basically the idea of thinking outside the box in an effort to always improve. Ironically, although it's one of my favorite qualities, I am not naturally creative. However, I love engaging people on our team that are, because of how important it is. Honestly, that's what matters. You don't have to be creative, but you just have to lead in a manner that encourages creativity. The goal should always be to improve, even when that involves risk-taking and implementing new ideas. With these risks comes an increased opportunity for failure. That's okay. Thinking outside the box does not always equal success at the moment. But it will likely lead to being a part of an innovative and exciting environment where people feel encouraged to bring their ideas to the table. Simon Sinek once said, "To succeed takes more than the desire to win. It also takes the acceptance that we could fail."[10] Failure is always a possibility, but it should never be a deterrent of new and bold ideas.

Let me add a little more perspective to this transformational quality. In the world of public safety, the "we've always done it this way" mentality often prevents our profession from engaging in innovation. Honestly, it can prevent us from implementing small, new ideas that could lead to big results. I am sure many of

---

[10] Sinek, Simon. "To Succeed Takes More than the Desire to Win. It Also Takes the Acceptance That We Could Fail." Twitter. Twitter, October 12, 2012. https://twitter.com/simonsinek/status/256746588322537472.

you reading this can relate, regardless of what kind of work you do. Limiting our teams in this area can be stifling and counter-productive. Yes, there is comfort in what we know, and often we prefer just staying in the status quo. It's safe and comfortable. Leaders that fall into this trap are never going to effectively move their organizations forward. Maintaining the status quo without a willingness to innovate can lead to unenviable results.

Blockbuster is a great example of this. When our kids were growing up, we spent time almost every weekend going to Blockbuster to get movies to rent. Great memories. Unfortunately, while Netflix was moving forward into the world of streaming, Blockbuster decided to stand firm right where they were. The results? I now go to streaming services to watch movies at home or on my iPad because renting DVDs is no longer an option.

As leaders, we need to be champions of creativity and outside-the-box thinking. It ensures we are always striving to get better, and it creates an environment that is conducive to employees feeling like they can bring their ideas to the table.

INDIVIDUALIZED CONSIDERATION

This final aspect of leadership ensures followers are developed and given opportunities for personal growth, and they are em-powered to make decisions.[11] In a nutshell, this is developing and empowering your people, which is discussed in chapter 5. One of our primary goals as leaders should always be to help our people grow. An employee that is valued through opportunities for growth and empowerment is more likely to have a strong allegiance to the organization. We invest in their development, they become more effective and impactful, more value is created for them, and their level of job satisfaction increases. Once again, this is extremely positive for all parties involved.

---

[11] Smith, Brien N., Ray V. Montagno, and Tatiana N. Kuzmenko. "Transformational and Servant Leadership: Content and Contextual Comparisons." SAGE Journals. JAI, September 14, 2016. https://journals.sagepub.com/doi/10.1177/107179190401000406.

Whether stated or not, almost all organizations have objectives and goals. Followers of transformational leaders experience a sense of empowerment by aligning their roles with those objectives and goals. They attach a greater sense of purpose (The second p of 3P leadership) to their roles, which results in extraordinary results. Unlike transactional leadership, which works toward ensuring certain performance standards are met, transformational leaders have the ability to inspire subordinates to exceed expectations. The original research related to this theory was based on the military, but later research has confirmed this style of leadership is effective in almost any organization or profession.[12]

In 2019, I conducted a police leadership research project which involved surveying Metro-Atlanta area police chiefs and officers at several different police departments. This study reinforced the results of other studies done on employee job satisfaction and organizational commitment. The research clearly demonstrated the more Metro-Atlanta police chiefs engaged in a transformational approach to leadership, the higher level of job satisfaction and employee commitment was realized by officers. Those officers working for chiefs that led with alternate approaches were not nearly as satisfied or committed.

Clearly, leadership absolutely must be about our people, and that is why I am such a believer in the transformational approach to leadership. If we fail to add value to our people, how can we expect them to add value to the company or community they serve?

PRACTICAL POINTS

The below picture is of one of our hallways on the second floor of our headquarters, which is home to our command staff. It serves as a reminder for all of us why we come to work every day. This question is a practical one we should ask ourselves daily:

---

[12] Bass and Riggio.

How can I add value to my people?

It could be the entire team, or it may be one person you are meeting with that day. It could be strictly business, or you may add value to someone struggling with a personal issue. Ultimately, making this question a part of your morning routine can help ensure a transformational mindset. Often, opportunities will arise throughout the day, but being intentional can ensure it remains a priority for you.

I am a task-list guy. I am constantly asking Siri to add things to my list, with reminder alerts for specific dates and times. One of the reasons I do this is simply to keep me from forgetting important tasks. Another reason I do it is so I can intentionally put "adding value to my people" tasks on that list. They stay on there until each task is completed. Regardless of how you ensure you complete important tasks, create a couple of reminders each day that correlate with intentional actions you can implement to add value to your people. Transformational leaders are intentional, and this is a simple, intentional step you can start with every day. By the way ... this also works for adding value to the important people in your life outside of work. Create reminders for yourself of things you can do for your family, friends, neighbors, etc.

PART TWO

3P LEADERSHIP— ADDING VALUE TO PEOPLE

"As you move up the leadership ladder, your perspective will change, as will your responsibilities. However, transformational leaders continue to ensure people are their number one priority, regardless of their position."

Chapter 3

IT'S ALL ABOUT PERSPECTIVE

THE BLUE JEAN Bandits. That's what they were known as. They were a group of guys that would go to a metro Atlanta mall, walk into one of the department stores, grab dozens of pairs of very expensive jeans and take off. I am talking thousands and thousands of dollars worth of jeans (they certainly were not stealing the kind of jeans I wear). They had hit several malls and were on the radar of mall security teams and police departments throughout the region. The mall in the city where I was a detective hired off-duty officers to sit in unmarked police cars during the evenings, hoping they could catch the Blue Jean Bandits in action. Easy job, easy money . . . so I thought.

There I sat in my tinted-out Dodge Intrepid in the parking lot of the mall near the department store that would be the likely target if they happened to show, which in my mind, was a very remote possibility. Mall security gave me one of their radios and asked me to listen while I sat in my car for five hours. I, of course, was on constant alert the entire time, watching every car that came in and out of the parking lot.

Okay . . . that's not really the case. I was actually watching movies on my portable DVD player while listening to mall security on the radio drone on and on about kids running through the food court and shoppers locking their keys in their cars.

As my shift at the mall was coming to an end, I suddenly

heard a high-pitch scream on the radio that was loud, but complete gibberish. I finally pieced together "They just hit Parisians and are getting in a dark SUV!" About that time, I observed an SUV speeding through the parking lot near me, with a mall security guy coming out yelling, "That's them!" I was able to catch up to their vehicle as they were exiting onto one of the main roads in our city where the mall was located. The chase was on.

The speed limit on this road was thirty-five mph, and we were quickly reaching speeds of up to eighty mph. I, of course, immediately got on the radio and advised what was happening. We weaved in an out of traffic, running red lights, and came to a major highway. As the suspects were getting on the northbound ramp, marked police cars joined in the chase. Now, our policy stated that an unmarked vehicle engaged in pursuit was to immediately disengage once marked units were there. So, I disengaged . . . sort of . . . as the pursuit continued northbound. Eventually, the suspects crossed the median, headed southbound, and crashed. Four suspects were immediately taken into custody. The driver was fifteen years old, and the other passengers were sixteen. We had one patrol car totaled, and another one that was badly damaged. Thankfully, no one was hurt.

Now, for Detective Robison, that was a night to remember! I helped capture the Blue Jean Bandits, and I got to be in a really cool chase. It was awesome. Over a decade later, Chief Robison has a very different perspective. The high-speed pursuit that I initiated endangered citizens on the road, myself, other officers, and even the suspects. What was the original charge that started all of this? Shoplifting.

My perspective now is that I do not believe it is worth endangering lives over property and minor traffic violations. In my current position, I have so much more to consider when making decisions than I did when I was an officer or detective. Just like my parent's perspective I referred to earlier, I see things differently than I did when I was chasing bad guys. The view has changed. My perspective has changed.

As I previously mentioned, I teach part-time for a national law enforcement training organization. As I travel all over the country, I love being around other public safety personnel and hearing about the good, the bad, and the ugly of what they are dealing with in their local departments. Although most departments face specific issues that are germane to the area they serve, I have found that we are all facing a lot of the same problems and struggles. Without fail, numerous problems I hear about are related to leadership, or should I say, lack of effective leadership. Don't get me wrong, it's not always a group of people slamming their supervisors (although that does happen). It is usually about legitimate gaps in leadership that we all deal with at one time or another, and some of those will be discussed in the next chapters.

One of the phrases I often hear is "they forgot where they came from." Translation: When people get promoted, they no longer care as much about the people they used to work with so closely. Or they used to be concerned about the people they worked with, and now they are more concerned about pleasing those above them, playing politics, and climbing their way to the top.

I seriously doubt that when people get promoted, one of their first goals is to completely disregard their former coworkers. Can you imagine, "I just got promoted and now it's my desire to completely screw over all of those men and women I used to work with every day." So, what's the problem? Well, some of the blame can certainly be put on those that have been promoted. Lack of preparation, ego, and motive are all contributors to bad leadership. But one of the greatest contributing factors is actually somewhat simplistic: it's a new role with a new perspective.

Each level in the organization has a different view. When I reference the top leader in an organization, I ascribe them the "thirty-thousand-foot view." This analogy is based on most commercial airline flights topping out around thirty thousand feet. That is typically as high as you will go, and when you look out the window, you can obviously see a lot more than what you initially viewed at ten thousand feet just after takeoff.

Let's relate this analogy to the typical city police department. A police officer normally has a ten thousand-foot view of how things work in a department. They are not typically exposed to high-level decision-making processes and don't often know why the organization operates a specific way. Mid-level supervisors, like Sergeants and Lieutenants, usually ascend to the fifteen thousand-to twenty thousand-foot view range. They often have greater exposure and some involvement in decisions being made and have a little more understanding of how things work operationally in the organization. Then you get to around twenty-five thousand feet for the command staff level, which is often comprised of Captains, Majors, Commanders, Deputy Chiefs, etc. They typically oversee most of the department's operations and should have a fairly strong grasp of not only what is occurring, but why. Finally, you have the Chief at the thirty-thousand-foot level, who should have a clear understanding of how the department operates overall, while also having a firm grasp of how the city in general functions, and some significant insight into the leadership perspectives and actions of the elected officials.

How about a small business analogy? I worked for a hometown bank when I was in college. This local bank consisted of one main branch, and two other smaller branches. Remember, this was a long time ago, well before online banking was invented. Tellers were the front-line employees at the ten-thousand-foot level. They dealt with the customers and were the faces of the bank. Each branch had a head teller that was basically a mid-level manager at the fifteen thousand-to-twenty-thousand-foot height. This person supervised all of the tellers and ensured effective customer service was being provided. I worked at one of the branches, and we had a branch manager who was around the twenty-five thousand foot view. She managed the entire branch and was very involved in the overall management of the entire banking operation. At the thirty-thousand-foot level, we had the bank president. He dealt with staff, customers, and other businesses throughout the community. The tellers had a very limited perspective compared to the bank president. The president I worked for started his banking career as a teller. Each time he was promoted to a new position, his view—his perspective—changed.

So, as people get promoted and move into new leadership roles, their view changes. The higher they go, the more their view expands. Those people they used to work with on the front line still have the same view and don't often comprehend the new responsibilities that correlate with the broader views. There are a few ways leaders can ensure their new roles do not create a disconnect with the people they are leading. These will be discussed in the next three chapters. From a broader perspective, leaders have to be vigilant in making sure their people are always a priority.

As you move up the leadership ladder, your perspective will change, as will your responsibilities. However, transformational leaders continue to ensure people are their number one priority, regardless of their position.

Using the police department example again, when an officer gets promoted to Sergeant, his/her number one priority should be the people on his/her shift. When a Lieutenant is promoted to Captain over an entire division, the people in each of the units he or she commands must be the priority. Perspectives change, prioritizing people should not. Specifically, for a patrol sergeant in my organization, that means always focusing first on the ten people he or she supervises. As these front-line supervisors lead and make decisions, they should always consider those ten people and how they are impacted. For me as Chief, regardless of what decision, change, or initiative I must implement, my primary focus must remain on the people in our organization. Are there other factors that should be considered? Absolutely. No matter how critical some of those factors may be, the police officers, firefighters, dispatchers, and administrative staff should always remain at the top of the list of factors to be considered when making decisions.

Important point: one of the main reasons leaders "forget where they came from" is often due to getting inundated with new tasks, processes, administrative duties, etc., in their new roles. We can easily lose sight of why we originally took on a leadership role in the first place, which was hopefully to increase the effectiveness of our organization and add value to our people. When we forget about the people, we forget about what's most important. The struggle is real. We can become overwhelmed by demands on our time, talents, and resources. Yet, top notch leaders consistently find a way to prioritize their people. Each new role brings a new perspective on the organization, but compelling force men and women are able to consistently focus on their greatest asset . . . their people.

The next chapters in this section discuss, in more detail, three specific areas in leadership that can ensure leaders keep a people-oriented perspective, regardless of what leadership role they acquire.

PRACTICAL POINTS

Do you have a common routine for decision-making? Maybe you use some sort of matrix, formal or informal. Do you have certain people you talk to and gather input from? Try to incorporate the following question and actions into your decision-making process. This can help ensure people remain the priority.

Who is this going to impact in our organization?

- Be intentional in creating opportunities for input from those who could be impacted.
- Once a final decision has been made, communicate it to those being impacted FIRST.
- Don't just tell them what has been decided, tell them why. Even if they don't like the decision, having an understanding of why the decision was made can make it easier.

Chapter 4

EVERYTHING STARTS
WITH ENGAGEMENT

ONE OF THE most important days in the history of our country, and the world for that matter, was June 6, 1944. D-Day. We all have seen the pictures of our young soldiers in Higgins' boats emptying onto the shores of Normandy, basically running into hell on earth. The bravery and sacrifices made that day are indescribable. Our society throws the word hero around a lot, but there is no greater example of heroes than the men involved in that horrifically difficult, and ultimately successful, military operation.

General Dwight D. Eisenhower was the Supreme Allied Commander in Europe, and the architect of the D-Day invasion. In the book, *How Ike Led: The Principles Behind Eisenhower's Biggest Decisions*, it's made clear the stress and difficulties the general endured in planning this invasion. Although the mission was extremely critical for success in the war, General Eisenhower clearly struggled with the toll he knew this would take on his soldiers. He was keenly aware there would be a lot of bloodshed and loss of life. Obviously, the view General Eisenhower had on the war, and the view of the soldiers was vastly different. Yet, Eisenhower never lost sight of the importance of those he was leading. This is obvious because of the time he took to engage with his men. He grasped the idea that keeping his people a priority meant spending time with them. In the military, it is easy for those with a twenty thousand- to thirty-thousand-foot view to look at soldiers as numbers and not people. Eisenhower did not allow that to happen to him.

General Eisenhower was responsible for approximately 156,000 soldiers in the Allied force. It was not humanly possible for him to spend time with each one of them individually. However, he made it a priority to engage with as many as possible. He did this by utilizing two approaches to engaging with his people. The first approach was strategically scheduling time with his men. The second approach was taking advantage of impromptu opportunities for engagement.

Eisenhower made it a priority in his schedule to meet with those he would be sending into battle. From the book:

> Schedule permitting, Ike spent as much time as he could visiting the men who would be executing the plan. He saw their morale as a critical input to success. During the buildup to the Normandy campaign Eisenhower visited twenty-two divisions, twenty-one airfields, and four major units of the naval fleet.

I can only assume General Eisenhower was a very busy man, with a lot of demands on his time. He could have easily tasked his commanders with handling meetings with the divisions, airfields, and naval fleet. But he didn't. Why? Based on my learning of his leadership approach described throughout the book, I would say it's because he understood the value of personally engaging with the people that mattered most, his soldiers.

He also created, or took advantage of, unscheduled moments of engagement. Another excerpt from the book:

> Later in the evening of June 5, Eisenhower began to make trips up and down the southern coast of England, visiting airborne troops. The late-summer

light was dimming, and C-47 transport planes, as well as the gliders and their tow planes, were moving into line. The dusk began to settle. The men stood in small groups near their planes, talking in low voices and smoking their cigarettes. Invariably Ike would drive up to each of these groups, get out of the car, and walk toward them. According to eyewitnesses, he'd flash that "magnificent smile" and encourage the troops to gather around him.

Did he talk about the mission and what was ahead? Was he ensuring the men were ready for battle? No . . . not at first, anyway:

A survivor of the war, Wallace Strobel, later told us of this encounter. "Where are you from?" Ike asked the tall paratrooper—number 23.

"From Michigan, Sir."

"How's the fly-fishing in Michigan?" General Eisenhower responded.

"It's great, Sir," Strobel replied.

Eisenhower went on to say that he had been to Michigan to fish on several occasions. After a discussion of this for a few minutes, the supreme Allied commander asked: "Are you ready and have you been briefed properly?"

"Yes, Sir, we've been well briefed, and we are ready."

"Good," Eisenhower said, and moved on to the next small group of paratroopers. Ike often added "Good luck" or "I know you are well prepared" as he left a gathering of men.

Years later, my father—a well-known military historian and his father's confidant—told *The Baltimore Sun*: "[Ike] was always trying to talk to troops about things back home, things that were familiar to them. If Ike found out that someone was from Kansas, he'd talk about cattle and farming, so it's natural that with Wally he discussed fishing."

Do you see what he was doing? He was making it about *them*. He was making it personal. And he wanted to confirm they had been led effectively, or "properly." A portion of his engagement was utilized to hear their perspective on the crucial task at hand.

Honestly, when it comes to being a transformational leader, everything starts with engagement. Do you want your people to trust you? It starts with engagement. Do you want credibility with your team? It starts with engagement. Do you want your people to feel valued? It starts with engagement. Do you want to have effective communication up and down the chain? It starts with engagement. Do you want to utilize your influence to be a compelling force in your organization? It starts with engagement. Conversely, people in leadership positions that sit in their office all day and avoid people are going to struggle with building trust, developing credibility, adding value to their people, creating effective communication, and being influential.

Maybe you are a strategic, organizational genius when it comes to managing your team. You may have years of experience and copious amounts of expertise. When it comes to institutional knowledge, you could be the best of the best. You might check all of the "effective management" boxes. Nevertheless, none of that will equate to you being an effective, compelling force leader if you don't devote yourself to your most valuable asset—your people. Devoting yourself to your people starts with spending time with them.

When I started as Chief in 2017 in my current department, I had to qualify with my assigned firearms, like all certified police officers have to do annually. It's a state requirement. I will never forget that day—not because of the actual shooting, but because of the reaction I observed when I arrived to qualify. When I pulled into the parking lot of the outdoor range we were using, there were already several officers on the range shooting. As I exited my vehicle and started working my way toward the range, there was a pause in the shooting, and for a few moments, people were awkwardly staring at me. As they went back to shooting, I asked someone why the awkward staring? The response was basically they had never seen a chief or other command staff members on the range with other officers. Now, this is not an uncommon practice at police agencies, so please don't take this as a criticism of the previous chief or anyone on the command staff at that time. Typically, the chief and command staff would have a "special" range day sometime in December because it was the end of the year and they had to get qualified before January 1. At our next leadership meeting, I instructed our command staff on the police side to sign up and qualify with the rest of our department from now on, as we would no longer have our training team set aside a day just for us. My thought was, I had been preaching we were all on the same team, and my actions needed to back that message.

I learned a valuable lesson from this experience. I learned the value of showing up, of spending time with our team, of continually engaging with the people in our department. I wish I could say that choosing to qualify like everyone else was an intentional, strategic approach to engagement. Honestly, it was not something I was even considering at that time. Ultimately, this experience served as a significant moment in my development as a leader. Any time I get to spend with our people is an opportunity to demonstrate their value to me and our organization.

I had a similar experience when I came to my first roll call soon after being hired. Roll calls happen before every shift. Supervisors and officers talk about what happened on the recent shift, things to be aware of, zone assignments, etc. It was a five p.m. roll call, and when I walked in, the loud and talkative room went silent. Unfortunately, this is not an uncommon dynamic in a lot of departments. When the chief or someone from command staff walks in roll call, everyone has the same question come to mind: "what's wrong?" That's not good, regardless of the profession.

When those in leadership roles drop in unexpectedly and the immediate vibe is "someone's in trouble" or "something must be wrong," that means leaders are not consistently engaging. These are the kind of gaps in leadership that prevent creating and maintaining a healthy culture. If you and I truly want to be a compelling influence on our people, we have to actually spend time with those people. Engagement truly matters. The first p in 3P leadership is not going to come to fruition without leaders making time with their people a priority.

PRACTICAL POINTS

We read about General Eisenhower practicing two forms of engagement, intentional and opportunistic. I have broken down some simple, effective engagement techniques in both categories that can help ensure you are placing the value on the people they deserve by giving them some of your time. Now, there are a couple of important caveats about these suggestions. First, when I say simple, I mean simple in theory. In theory, there is not a lot to meeting and talking to people. The problem is most of us are extremely bogged down timewise, and it's hard to imagine adding anything else to our already full days. You may have to step back and reexamine your priorities. As previously discussed, our people should be at the top of our priority list, and you may have to implement some adjustments to your daily task list and calendar. Some of you are reading this and thinking this is simply not possible. You have a great deal of responsibilities. I get it. This won't happen overnight. It will take some time to get into more of an engagement routine. Even then, you may be very limited in how much time you can devote to this, but you must start somewhere.

Also, if you have never really been a leader that engages and you just all of a sudden start showing up, don't expect immediate, positive results. Remember those awkward moments I described? Expect some of those moments at the beginning of your engagement journey. It could take a while to get into a groove for you and your people. Give it time.

" Remember, adding value to people with purpose and passion has to start with building a foundation through engagement. **"**

Intentional Engagement

1) Schedule time on your calendar to visit your teams, units, shifts, etc. Block off time and don't let anything beyond an emergency interrupt that time. It's up to you whether or not you let people know you're coming ahead of your arrival. At first, that's what I did, but now I typically drop in unannounced. Also, don't come with an agenda. I had a deputy chief at one time that asked everyone he spoke to, "Is there anything I can do for you?" He meant it. At first, it just seemed like he was being nice, but eventually, people realized he really wanted to hear from them. This is a great question to ask when you are spending time with your people in groups (or anytime for that matter).

I'll give you an example of how I apply this in my job. We have six fire stations, and we have three twenty-four-hour fire shifts. In order for me to visit all of our fire suppression personnel, I need to go to each station three different times, for a total of eighteen visits. That's a lot, and it's not something I can necessarily do quickly. So, I keep a chart of all three shifts and six stations. Let's say I go by Station 1 on A shift. I'll go in and shoot the breeze a little and ask how they are doing, if there is anything I can do for them, etc. I also ask if they have any questions or if there is anything I can address (this correlates with our communication topic in chapter 6). I have had visits last no longer than ten minutes, and I have had them last over an hour.

Also, always be sure you let them know how much you appreciate them. Words do matter. Don't ever miss an opportunity to build up your people. As a matter of fact, if you get a chance, find a couple of examples of some good work the people you are visiting have recently done and make a big deal about it when you drop by to see them. Being able to offer specific examples related to your showing appreciation adds more meaning to your words.

By the way, firefighters are excellent cooks, so I have learned the value of coming by at mealtime! Because they have gotten used to me coming by, I'll now get invitations to breakfast or dinner at stations from time to time. It's a win-win!

2) Attend scheduled trainings, meetings, luncheons, etc. for employees when appropriate. Again, if you have never done it before, they are going to wonder why in the world you are there. Eventually, they will get used to it. Sometimes, I'll go to a training class simply to show them my support, spend a few minutes there, and then leave. Know the room. If your being there for a long period of time is going to be counterproductive to whatever it is they are doing, go by a few minutes before, and maybe even briefly address the team if appropriate at the beginning. "I appreciate you all continuing to work hard toward taking care of our clients," or, "You all are the best of the best, and a big part of that is your willingness to participate in training like this." Our officers have quarterly in-service training, and I typically try to sign up for one of the scheduled days.

There will also be times when fully committing to immersing yourself into your employee's world will substantially increase your credibility. I have a full set of fire turnout gear. I'm honestly not sure why, but I keep it in the back of my truck. Trust me, if any of our citizens were counting on me to put out a fire at their house, they would be gravely disappointed, as their house would burn to the ground. Nonetheless, I had a conversation with one of our fire training officers, and he convinced me it would be very beneficial for me to go to live fire training and actually put on my turnout gear and participate. So, that's exactly what I did. I suited up and followed the training officer during each scenario inside the burning building, and I loved it! I also learned more about the intricacies of their job, and the team appreciated me prioritizing my time to be part of their world. Sometimes, doing what they do can send a message that you are interested in what's going on in their world, and you are all on the same team.

3) Schedule breakfast/lunch/coffee with your people. If you have a small company, schedule a "meeting" with your entire company and let them know you are bringing food and/or coffee. If you work for a larger organization, do this with different teams. This creates a three-for-one opportunity. You are engaging, you are showing your appreciation for them, and you can also use these gatherings for some intentional communication and feedback.

Opportunistic Engagement

1) Develop habits that increase the likelihood of creating opportunities to engage with your people. For example, when going from your office to the parking lot, walk through areas you know you will likely see others (bosses are notorious for strategically avoiding people as they come and go). We have two parking lots at our headquarters. The front parking lot is the public lot and is also where the majority of our civilian and administrative staff park, due to a more direct route to their offices. Our back parking lot is the secured lot, where officers, detectives, and other personnel park. When I started my current job, one of our Lieutenants (now a Captain) gave me some great advice. He told me that if I parked in the back lot, it would give me more opportunities to engage with our front-line personnel. Genius! I have done it ever since, and he was right. Who knew that where I chose to park would enhance my ability to be a compelling force leader!

There is another quick example that almost anyone can do. Most mornings, I get in my office, get my coffee, and then walk the entire upstairs to say good morning to everyone. If time allows, I'll stop and chat about the weather, the game on Saturday (Go Dawgs!), their families, etc. Sometimes those conversations morph into work, but not always. Often, it's short and sweet, but it's a habit I have developed that helps get me in front of some of our staff.

2) At times, having an "open door policy" can be challenging. We all have a lot of work to get done, and interruptions can alter accomplishing important tasks. However, there is value in establishing a reputation where people really do feel comfortable dropping in, which can create tremendous opportunities for engagement. If you have work that needs to be completed, close your door. There is nothing wrong with that. Just don't be one of those leaders that works behind a closed door all day. Your intentions may be to simply get the job done, but the message you are sending is that you have no interest in interacting with your team. When the door is open, be prepared to engage. When people come by, put down your phone, push away your laptop, and make them feel like the most important person in the world. If you simply don't have the time at that moment, be honest and tell them, and ask them if you can schedule a time with them later in the day, or the next couple of days, so you can give them the time and attention they deserve.

I want to finish this chapter with a message to those of you that are reading this and thinking there is no way you have this kind of time for engagement. I have been there. When I first became a Chief, my focus was on "effectively running the department." That was my job, and that was my focus. I can also recall periods where I felt like I was running around with my hair on fire, and there was not enough time in the day to get everything I needed to get accomplished, much less spend time conversing with people. Some of you may have other types of engagement roadblocks to overcome. You may have a boss that does not value people like you do, and he or she may make it extremely challenging for you to give time to the people on your team that deserve it the most. Also, you may be an introvert, and just thinking of spending so much time with people makes you want to curl up in a corner and take a nap. At my core, I am an introvert. Remember emotional labor? A lot of engagement absolutely drains me.

Once I learned how important engagement is, as it relates to connecting with our employees and creating a healthy culture, I had to take ownership of my weaknesses and make some adjustments. I encourage you to take a step back and do an honest assessment of your day-to-day leadership approach. Have a courageous conversation with yourself.

If you are a micromanager, you are not going to have time to spend with your people because you are too busy trying to accomplish everything yourself (and you are likely making your people miserable). If that's you, own it and start changing it.

You may be terrible at time management. If that's you, own it and get help prioritizing your time and tasks.

If you are an introvert, you just have to make yourself do it. Take it from someone who has been there . . . the more you do it, the easier it gets. When you know you are going to be spending time with people, as an introvert, it helps to create a game plan regarding topics of conversation, intentional friendliness, etc.

And, if you have one of those bosses I mentioned that stifles your ability to influence through engagement, have a courageous conversation with him or her. Do some research on transformational leadership (or just use what I shared in this book). Demonstrate how the new approach you desire to implement in your leadership role will ultimately result in employees experiencing a higher level of job satisfaction and commitment to the organization. Remember, adding value to *people* with *purpose* and *passion* has to start with building a foundation through engagement.

During the first few months of 2020, we were reminded of the importance of the men and women serving on the front lines of our hospitals. The physical, mental, and emotional toll these medical workers endured while caring for Covid patients—many of which did not survive—was more than most people are wired to handle. Hospitals in the state of New York were especially impacted by the pandemic. It is estimated that Covid has been responsible for over forty thousand deaths in New York state.

Michael J. Dowling is the president and chief executive officer of Northwell Health, the largest healthcare provider in New York. With a total workforce of more than seventy-six thousand employees, Northwell is the state's largest private employer. The healthcare provider has twenty-three hospitals and more than 830 outpatient facilities, including 220 primary care practices, fifty-two urgent care centers, home care, rehabilitation, and end-of-life care services.

During Covid, Dowling could have provided several good reasons not to engage with his people—he didn't have time, as he was too busy leading his company through a crisis. The company needed him, and he couldn't risk getting exposed to Covid. He leads seventy-six thousand people—there is no way he can even think about spending time with all of those employees . . . there are too many!

And yet, he did just that. Dowling, understanding the importance of being with his people during a crisis, met with staff at all twenty-three hospitals. He wanted to actually spend time with those that were placing so much on the line each day they came to work. The message he wanted to convey was that leadership was with them, and they would get through this together.

This will blend into the topic of communication a little later in the book, but engagement is never more important than when times are tough. You want to lead effectively in a crisis? Show up and spend time with your team. Sometimes, we as leaders feel like we need to provide great ideas and insight on how to manage whatever difficulty our team may be enduring. Unfortunately, that is not always plausible. We don't always have the answers but being present can often be more impactful than offering tidbits of wisdom. Tell them what you know, answer what you can, but most importantly, be there. Be seen. Be available. Be a leader. Engage.

Chapter 5

CRITICAL COMMUNICATION

WORDS MATTER. DURING my senior year in high school, I put on a little weight. Although I was a pretty active soccer player, I, for whatever reason, had gotten a little heavier. A "friend" of mine—who will remain nameless—decided to create a new nickname for me in honor of my minor (at least in my mind) weight gain. He started calling me "Dex." Dex was short for Dexatrim, a popular weight loss pill in the eighties. The guy who had referred to me as Johnny since middle school was now finding great delight in calling me Dex.

Fast forward just over twenty years, and I was now working as a Lieutenant in the same department I now serve as Chief. Our city has a large concert venue with approximately seven thousand covered seats, and five thousand general admission seats on a lawn. I, like many of our officers, worked off-duty security at concerts, and I often had an assignment on the lawn. When officers work on the lawn, their primary role is to try to keep the peace and deal with patrons that are a little too rowdy or out of control—especially after consuming copious amounts of alcohol, marijuana, or other behavior-altering substances (I always left those jobs wreaking of marijuana and craving Cheetos!).

One of those nights I worked the lawn detail, a large skirmish broke out. As you can imagine, when the lights are out and a band is performing, it is dark on the lawn. Basically, our goal during most incidents was to grab those involved, get them out of the crowd and implement one of three options. If they immediately calmed down and weren't overly inebriated or high, we would give them a warning and let them go back. If they were too out of control, we would document the incident and remove them from the venue. Finally, if they could not get their act together and wanted to fight the police, the venue staff, and anyone else in their way, they found themselves in the back of a patrol car on the way to jail.

Once this particular fight started, we got to the group and started grabbing those involved. I grabbed one guy and pulled him out of the crowd and started escorting him to our security office. As we were moving, the guy all of a sudden looked at me and said, "Johnny? Johnny Robison, is that you?" I looked at his face and immediately recognized him as my old nickname-loving-friend from high school.

I immediately said his name back, but you want to know the first question that came to my mind over twenty years later? "Don't you mean Dex?" I had not thought once about him, and that was my very first thought. Words matter.

By the way . . . when this happened, we would have both been in our late thirties. I was in pretty good shape at that point, and he probably had a good twenty to thirty pounds on me at that time. Yes, I did take some pleasure in the obvious difference in our physiques. And, for those of you wondering, I talked to him for a few minutes and let him go back and enjoy the show. I know for a fact, if some of you reading this had been in my place, you would have locked him up!

Emily Dickenson once said, "I know nothing in the world that has as much power as a word." Zig Ziglar stated, "There is power in words. What you say is what you get." In the book of James in the Bible, a very strong description is given regarding the power of words. James 3:3–6a states, "When we put bits into the mouths of horses to make them obey us, we can turn the whole animal. Or take ships as an example. Although they are so large and are driven by strong winds, they are steered by a very small rudder wherever the pilot wants to go. Likewise, the tongue is a small part of the body, but it makes great boasts. Consider what a great forest is set on fire by a small spark. The tongue also is a fire . . ." That first part of verse six comparing our words to "fire" provides a vivid description regarding how powerful and potentially destructive our communication can be.

Power and words go hand in hand, and this is especially true in leadership. I often share with our leadership team a truth I learned a long time ago. The higher up you go in the organization, the more people hang on your every word. Tony Robbins shared his thoughts on the correlation between words and leadership when he said, "Throughout human history, our greatest leaders and thinkers have used the power of words to transform our emotions, to enlist us in their causes, and to shape the course of destiny. Words cannot only create emotions, they create actions. And from our actions flow the results of our lives." Words being used to transform followers . . . that is what effective leaders do.

Whether written or verbal, words are obviously needed for communication. What makes communication effective is when those words are presented or received with a purpose that is greater than simply trying to ensure a message is understood by the listener or reader. Compelling force, transformational leaders grasp the ability to enhance employee satisfaction and organizational commitment through the transparent presentation and reception of information, thoughts, and ideas on a consistent basis. I can promise you that if you show me an organization with a healthy culture where employees appreciate being valued, I'll show you an organization where leaders emphasize the importance of effective communication up and down the chain. Quality, culture-building communication is more than typing words in an email or verbalizing quarterly goals in a sales meeting. Transformational communication taps into the power of words with the intention of creating an environment where employees feel like they are an important part of the team because they are informed, and they are heard.

I firmly believe communication is one the most important

characteristics of leadership, and yet it is the one area we often fail at the most. Failing to communicate in a manner that results in adding value to our people can be attributed to several possibilities. Some leaders simply don't know how to effectively communicate. For many of us, this trait does not come naturally.

I am sure many of you are familiar with the DISC behavioral assessment. This tool takes a deep dive into aspects of people's personality and is especially beneficial in seeing how people work with others. It's a great tool that can be used to help improve teamwork and communication. Individuals with "D" personalities are typically get-it-done, results-oriented people. "I" personalities are very relational and exceed in influencing others. "S" personalities are great teammates that often are not in the limelight but are extremely dependable. "C" personalities place a great deal of emphasis on details and accuracy.

I am a high D. The natural communication style for a D is to keep communication short and sweet—straight to the point, give the basic facts, and move on to the next topic. Now, if two people talking are both high Ds, communication will likely be seamless. But if I am talking to a high I, S, or C, and I stick to my high D approach, my effort to effectively communicate will likely crash and burn. Some of us are just not naturally gifted when it comes to implementing creative communication. One of the reasons for this is we often fail to adapt our communication style when communicating with people that are wired differently.

Another possibility for failure can be related to the amount of effort and time it takes to implement effective, two-way communication. Transformational communication is hard work! Honestly, it often feels like a never-ending job. Just when I think I have communicated effectively, I sometimes realize I still have a long way to go. We often prioritize it in our mind, but we get busy. Before we know it, our intentionality in this area wanes, and we get caught up in all the other day-to-day minutia of our roles. Some leaders know it's important, but they can't figure out how to prioritize it on a consistent basis.

Remember the joke I shared earlier about autocratic leadership being easier? That's especially the case when it comes to communication. "I'm the boss. I tell you what to do, and you simply do it. There is no need for context or transparency, and I certainly don't have the time or need to listen to what you think or feel. The information you receive is the information you need to do your job."

I once taught a leadership session at a large police department's leadership retreat. I sat through a couple of hours of hearing the chief talk to his command staff — which consisted of approximately forty people. He went on and on about how this was their department, and how much he desired their input. Yet, I watched him completely hammer people that shared anything that may have been contrary to his ideas on leading the department. Ultimately, he disregarded input and made it very apparent his agenda should be their agenda. That is a clear example of autocratic leadership, and although that approach is much easier for the leader, it is detrimental to the overall well-being of the organization.

Leaders that prioritize their people prioritize creating trust and buy-in through intentional, consistent communication. If we want to ensure our people feel like they matter, we demonstrate that through sharing and listening. Just like in my marriage, I can tell my wife all day that I love her and appreciate her. However, when I fail her in the area of communication, I am not demonstrating how much I value her through my actions. Just like at work, communication is also hard in marriage, and it must be a priority in order to have a healthy, fulfilling marriage. Harvard Professor of Business Administration and leadership author Nitin Nohria was straight and to the point when he stated, "Communication is the real work of leadership."

That is so true. I have found that other effective leadership approaches are very limited without having a firm foundation of communication to build everything else upon.

There have been numerous books written on communication. I have read some of them, and you probably have too. You may have learned some effective methods to enhance the process of sharing and receiving information. But if you don't consistently prioritize effective, two-way communication in your area of influence, those effective methods will likely dissipate and become less of an importance. I hope this section will inspire and equip you to keep communication a focal point in your leadership toolbox. Maybe you already know how important this topic is, but you have lost your way in making what was once a priority no longer a reality in your organization. I would love for this to help you create a blueprint for realigning your priorities with communication being toward the top of your list of what matters most (remember . . . if we value our people, our communication will reflect that value).

Maybe you are like me, and creativity is not one of your strong suits. Ideally, you will be able to implement some of the proven communication ideas that are provided in this section. If you don't feel like these ideas align with your current circumstances, hopefully my take on communication will help spur some creative communication strategies that will work well in your environment.

Let me throw out one important caveat here. Effective communication is hard work and, much like leadership in general, it is an infinite game. There will never be a point where you can declare "mission accomplished." You must understand that you will always have to work hard in this area. Even if you have mastered many effective techniques as a leader, getting everyone else on board is a completely different challenge. I can honestly say transformational communication has consistently been one of my highest priorities. Have we seen a lot of improvement? I believe our people would tell you yes. But we still have a long way to go. It can be extremely frustrating at times, but don't give up! When a leader recognizes the importance of getting communication right, that leader is demonstrating they grasp what matters.

Let's look at two-way communication and discuss some strategic ideas on how to have a healthy culture that is built upon impactful communication.

DOWN THE CHAIN

We will maintain a thirty-thousand-foot view for the two main directions of communication . . . down the chain (communication from leaders to the people) and up the chain (from the people to the leaders). Following these two sections, we will then dive into an entire chapter of "Practical Points" that will provide several ideas you can easily implement for your unit, team, department, or organization. When we talk about "down the chain," we are talking about communication coming from the leaders to the team members. Like a coach to his or her players, or a teacher to his or her students, a basic function of leadership is the person in charge sharing information with the people needing that information to successfully do their jobs. However, if we want to be a compelling force in our roles as leaders, we will realize that the effective dissemination of information allows us to do so much more for our people than give them the basics to do their jobs. When we, as leaders, consistently communicate with our people, we can:

Add value to employees by keeping them in the know

Knowledge is power, and knowledge creates a sense of worth. Your people will feel like they matter when they know what's happening. It's really that simple. When we make an effort to ensure our people stay consistently informed, they are more likely to stay engaged. The "knowledge is power" approach is often used by people in leadership positions through leveraging information as a means to obtain more power and authority. That takes us back to autocratic leadership. Leaders who hoard information will not earn trust or credibility, and they keep their people in the dark. Guess what . . . if it's important to you, it's probably important to them. Actually, I have discovered that information I felt was not that important was indeed important to some of the people on our teams. A good rule of thumb . . . you can rarely share too much. Yes, there are times we simply cannot share, but that is typically rare unless you work in some top secret, "If I tell you, I will have to kill you," type of job. Leaders that end up being nothing more than bad bosses are notorious for hoarding information. The more I do my job, the more I realize I really can share almost everything with my people. The more I do my job, the more I realize I should share almost everything with my people.

Create an opportunity to share the why

We are often guilty of giving the what without the why. However, the why is often more important than the what when it comes to adding value to our people. When we communicate information, we should be intentional in also providing proper context. For example, if we are making an organizational change, we should not only effectively communicate what that change is, but also how it will impact our people and why the change is being made. Even if they don't agree with the change, if you tell them the why, that will potentially help them get on board with the change moving forward. In our Practical Points chapter on communication, I will use the implementation of our new pursuit policy as a practical example of how to communicate change with your people. I can assure you that one of the most important aspects of redeveloping that policy was providing my reason for executing those changes. There are still several people that disagree with the new policy, but they at least understand my convictions that led to creating it.

Keep what's important in front of our people

As we will see a little later in the book, one of the keys to being a purpose-driven organization is leadership's constant communication of the organization's mission, values, purpose, etc. It's amazing how often we have opportunities to integrate reminders of what we value as a team in our day-to-day communication. Culture-oriented leaders communicate consistently what's important. Even with the simple emails we send relaying pertinent information, we can create a nexus between the topic and important values in our culture.

Consistently show appreciation

We can never do this enough. There is always value in demonstrating gratitude toward those we depend on to get the job done. Staff meetings, drop-ins, impromptu gatherings, emails, video chats, one on one conversations . . . these are all avenues we can use to communicate information, and each time we do so, we need to also view these interactions as opportunities to tell our people how much we appreciate them. When possible, be intentional and be specific. When you are preparing an agenda for a meeting, find some "good job" examples and share them. Look for ways you can brag about your team when sending out an email to them about a recent change in the organization. If you know you are having a one-on-one with someone, always be prepared to talk about something they do well and share with them what a value they are to the team. It seems so simple, yet leaders can consistently add value to their teams by proactively looking for ways to show appreciation, and this is often possible through the various ways we communicate with our people.

UP THE CHAIN

This aspect of communication is not easy. I can honestly say I feel like I have been screaming my desire for input up the chain from the mountaintop for years. I am consistently telling people at all levels I want to hear from them, and sometimes, it's still crickets. It has immensely improved, but this continues to be a learning process. It's funny how we often hear that people want more input, and yet can also be hesitant to give it. Employees want to feel like they are contributing and bringing value to the team.

I played basketball in middle school, and some in high school. I was not very good. I busted my butt in practice and worked really hard, but come game time, I took my place on the bench. Unfortunately, that's exactly where I spent most of my "illustrious" basketball career. I once had a high school coach tell me that if his other players had my heart and hustle, they would be unstoppable. That was just another way of telling me that I was a hard worker with very little talent. I appreciated the sentiment, nonetheless. I truly loved my middle school coach. He was a great coach and an even greater man. The gym we played in back in the eighties was torn down several years later so a new one could be built. Coach grabbed pieces of the court we all played on and gave those pieces to many of his former players, including me. I loved the gesture, but I joked with him that he should have saved a piece of the bench for me because I spent a lot more time there than I ever did on the court.

People in our organizations should never feel like they are on the bench. Now, don't get me wrong, we all have some that choose to be there. But those employees that want to feel like what they do matters need to know their job is crucial to the mission of the organization. One of the ways leaders ensure that happens is by intentionally creating opportunities for them to share input, questions, and concerns up the chain. Saying we have an open-door policy is not enough to ensure that occurs. As I said, people are often hesitant to proactively provide input. Why? Well, part of it is simply the perception that it is not their place to share their ideas with those in charge. This is especially true in public safety, where traditionally there is a strong adherence to a chain of command. This command structure is important and has its place, but I have worked hard to change some of the negative perceptions that are associated with a paramilitary structure. Yet, there are still people in our organization that don't feel comfortable talking to the "brass" because you just don't do that.

Others may be hesitant because they have seen or experienced the rejection of input from leaders in the past. Some bosses make it very clear they have no interest in hearing from their people.

Others, like in the example I shared earlier in this chapter, talk about wanting input but then demonstrate with their actions that it's nothing more than lip service. It does not take long for people to decide it's just not worth putting their heads on a chopping block to share ideas. That is NOT what a healthy culture resembles.

Leadership must be intentional and consistent when it comes to soliciting input from all levels of the organization. Like almost every leadership tenet we discuss in this book, if this is not something you have done before, it will take time to change employee perception regarding your desire to hear from them. When you start implementing some of the ideas listed in the next chapter, don't expect immediate results. Regardless, stay consistent and share the success stories of how employee input was not only welcomed, but how it positively impacted the team or organization. When employees have opportunities to communicate up the chain, the following can happen:

Your organization will get better

So simple, yet so true. When one person, or a handful of people, make most of the decisions based on what they know, this will not likely result in the most effective outcomes. More people equal more experience and more ideas. More experience and more ideas equal better decisions. This is especially the case when you have an opportunity to engage staff members that have experience or expertise in a specific area.

There is a lot that goes into purchasing a fire truck. Fire apparatuses are highly technical and complex. When it comes to making decisions on purchasing a new ladder truck or engine, it only makes sense to get the actual firefighters involved since they drive or use these tremendous vehicles as a daily part of their job. They are the experts, and they are the ones that ultimately have to live with whatever we choose. Therefore, they should have input on decisions related to purchasing and equipping fire trucks.

You get great ideas

I continue to be amazed at how smart and talented the people are in our organization. I especially love it when they think outside the norm. As I said before, we tend to get stuck in the status quo mentality of "we have always done it this way," which can be a killer of innovation. If we did not have a culture where people felt comfortable sharing their input and ideas, we would miss out on so much! We have people with backgrounds in technology, social work, accounting, construction, and engineering. They bring so much to the table that makes us better.

You create buy-in from your people

When your employees know they are valued and have skin in the game, they will have much more of an allegiance to the mission and the organization in general. Remember the nexus between transformational leadership and organizational commitment? A big part of that is when employees realize they are an important part of the team, they will be more committed to the team being successful.

Problems get addressed

Leaders can't address problems they don't know exist. This can also be caused by leaders that are completely disengaged from their organization. However, if employees work in an environment where problems exist (which is in every organization), and have no hope of those problems getting addressed, the result is a blow to morale. Resentment and frustration can build, and before you know it, you are leading a group of disgruntled employees.

When employees know there are avenues they can utilize to make leadership aware of problems, and they feel their concerns are validated by leaders that are willing to listen, the results will be much more positive—especially when legitimate issues are brought to light and addressed. Even if the outcome is not what an employee was hoping for, the investment of time toward that employee from leadership will certainly add value because of how it was handled.

General Colin Powell once said, "The day soldiers stop bringing you their problems is the day you have stopped leading them." That is a powerful statement that brings home the strong correlation between leadership and hearing from our people.

"There is always value in getting in front of your people to communicate pertinent information and provide a game plan moving forward when emotions are high."

Chapter 6

CRITICAL COMMUNICATION —
PRACTICAL POINTS

I AM WRITING this chapter on a Sunday, the day before I have my first of many scheduled annual survey meetings at six a.m. For the next month, I will spend hours meeting with all of our teams, discussing the input they provided on a department-wide survey that was sent out last month. The good news? There were a lot of comments about how much communication has improved. The bad news? There were a lot of comments about how much communication needs to still be improved! As I have said, communication is an infinite game, and it's hard work. I am a realist, and I know we still have much to do in this area. However, I can say with confidence that many of the practical ideas I share in this chapter have made two-way communication in our organization much more effective. Some ideas have worked better than others, but I do believe our intentionality is working. I can promise you, when we fail in this area, we usually hear about it. But that's good! That means people are providing input.

Some of these suggestions can be directly copied and immediately implemented. Other ideas you may need to tweak for your specific team or organization.

Please note, these tools can be used by CEOs, mid-level managers, front-line supervisors, or training personnel. Again, there may need to be some tweaking involved, but you can take the core idea and make it work in your area of influence. Even if you don't use any of these specific ideas, I hope it will get your creative juices flowing and help you and your people develop a communication strategy that will add value to your people and organization. When intentionally engaging in communication, don't forget to take advantage of the opportunity to praise your people, especially when it can be done publicly. Compelling force communication takes advantage of opportunities to show appreciation for our team members.

DOWN THE CHAIN

Give Them the *Why*

This part is a little broader and can be implemented in some of the other suggestions described throughout this section. It is important to be intentional about telling your people the *why* and not just the *what*. For example, if simple information is being given in an email, add a few lines detailing why the action described is necessary. As I said before, there is very little you can't share with your people. The same goes for in-person sharing. Tell them the *why* when giving them the *what*.

When it is something especially significant, or something you know is going to create some waves, make time to meet with everyone and give them the *why* in detail. You might even have some examples or a story to tell to help drive the *why* home. Remember when I said I changed our pursuit policy and made it stricter? I knew this was not going to go over well, so after sending out the new policy for review, I set up meetings with all police personnel and shared my strong conviction on not endangering our officers or the public in pursuits that involved minor traffic violations or property crimes. I shared my Blue Jean Bandit pursuit story and my new perspective on when a pursuit should occur. Did they all 100 percent agree with the new policy? Absolutely not. Did they all know my *why* and the conviction behind it? Yes. Does that matter? Absolutely.

I'll give one more example that is a little unusual. In the past, when someone was terminated, an email was sent to the entire department simply stating that the employee was no longer employed with the agency. Guess what happened about ten seconds after the email was sent to all personnel? The rumor machine hit warp speed, and as usual, most of the information being spread was not remotely accurate. Now, when a termination takes place, we set up meetings with the appropriate department and share what led to the termination. I always start by saying that I, in no way, want to speak badly of a former employee. That's not the goal. We are a team, and the goal is for everyone to be informed of what exactly led to having to let someone go. I may not always get specific with details, but people walk away understanding what happened and why an employee is no longer with us. This practice has been well received, and it has helped reduce fears of "leadership is out to get us" when they find out exactly what led to a dismissal.

Video Chats

Want an easy way to get the same message out to all employees in the organization? Create a video message and send it out to everyone. It can be as simple as creating a video on an iPhone, or you can go full production mode if you have the resources to do so. Either way, it can be informative while also being a more personal mode of communication because it's you talking! It does not take long, and you can do it regularly, or you can do it when circumstances necessitate a message from you. I would advise keeping it short and sweet. The longer the video, the less likely you will get people to watch it.

My version of this is called Chief's Chat. I try to create one every four to six weeks. I keep a list on my phone of topics I will cover the next recording. I have had some talented people on my staff help me make it fun from time to time, like in December when it looked like I was filming from the North Pole. Funny or not, the goal is always to address important topics. Even if some of the information may be a little more specific to one department, I have found that people like knowing what's going on in other parts of the organization as well as their own.

Hot Topic Meetings

When a change, incident, or crisis reaches a certain level, schedule meetings with staff to address those topics. This is another reason why engagement is so important. Spending time with your people can help you sense when it's time to address topics that are making waves on your team or in your organization.

Our entire city recently received some unexpected raises to help stay competitive in the market and show appreciation for our employees. However, because of several factors, one of our divisions in public safety got much less of an increase than the other two divisions. As you can imagine, that did not go over well with the one division that received less. This quickly became an extremely hot topic that created a lot of emotion, so I set up specific meetings and met with all personnel to provide the *why* and address their concerns. Was everyone happy after these meetings? Not at all. They had some deep-seated anger and frustration, which I totally understood. Regardless, there is always value in getting in front of your people to communicate pertinent information and provide a game plan moving forward when emotions are high.

Annual Meetings

The President of the United States has State of the Union meetings. We call our annual meeting the State of the Department. Usually, in March, we meet for an hour to discuss the upcoming year, our strategic plan for that particular year, and any other topics that are of interest to our employees. I also try to take advantage of this time to emphasize the importance of our mission and values. We allow plenty of time for questions, and we feed them breakfast or lunch. These meetings are recorded and made available to everyone. When you have employees working shifts, especially nights, you are going to have some that cannot attend. That is why it's important to record it so everyone can have the chance to see what was presented.

Share Pertinent Documents

When there is documentation available to support what's being shared information-wise, share it. When referring to this year's strategic plan, email it to everyone. When talking about the newly adjusted pay ranges, provide access for everyone to actually see the new pay structure. Don't just talk about the budget, provide a copy. If you made changes to the organizational chart, send the updated version to all personnel and post it in public spaces for everyone to see. Similar to the information we share verbally or in writing, there is very little we cannot share with our people, documentation-wise.

Regular Virtual/Phone Sessions

Have a regular, set time once a week, bi-weekly, monthly, etc., where people know they can log or call in and get regular updates. Timely information can be shared, and if this is done on a regularly set schedule, each session should not take long. You definitely want to keep these short and sweet, or people will quickly lose interest. Employees can choose whether or not they want to participate, but they all will know that, for example, every Tuesday at eleven a.m., they can hop on a virtual meeting, or dial in, and get the latest and greatest information on what's happening. I have to give credit to two of our fire executive leaders for coming up with this smart idea.

Newsletters

This is old school, but it still works. Regular publications can include a variety of information detailing scheduled events, important updates, personnel moves, new hire profiles, monthly stats, etc. This can be an effective tool for quality communication, and the goal is to do it consistently, so employees get to a point where they expect it. Newsletters can easily be done through department-wide emails, and technology has created other avenues for scheduled communication through personal devices and apps.

Multilocation Digital Signage

Speaking of technology . . . you can now have TVs/monitors in several different locations that share whatever information you feel is important. It does cost some money, but it is easy to set up and facilitate. I'll use my current department as an example. Imagine having a TV in every fire station, one on each floor of headquarters/police, and one in our 911 center. We can easily provide department-wide content, including the latest Chief's Chat, profiles of our most recent hires, information on our next promotional ceremony and other scheduled events, and shoutouts to some personnel that just received lifesaving awards.

At the same time, we could also post specific information to the fire stations regarding next month's fire training schedule while also providing a "save the date" for our 911 appreciation week and activities on the television in our dispatch center. Additionally, we could also share last month's police stats on the television in the roll call room at HQ. The options are limitless, and it is easy to ensure what's being shared is up-to-date and relevant.

UP THE CHAIN

Scheduled and Impromptu Engagement

As detailed before, engagement is one of the foundations of transformational leadership. When we consistently engage, we can add value, build trust/credibility and connect with our people. It is also an opportunity to receive input from employees. The more you are around, the more they will feel comfortable sharing questions and concerns.

Remember when General Eisenhower was engaging with his men before D-Day and asked, "Are you ready, and have you been briefed properly?" He wanted to hear from them. He could have simply provided whatever information he felt was pertinent at the time and wished them good luck. Yet he also provided them an opportunity to share if they felt ready and had been provided an effective briefing about the mission.

When I am with personnel at a roll call, fire station, or on the floor of our 911 center, I try to always ask if they need anything or have any questions. I will also often ask if there are any rumors I need to confirm or deny in a joking manner. I am seriously hoping they will share what they are hearing so I can properly address what's being said. It's just another way of trying to capture what's on their mind. I can honestly say that I have done this enough that several people now feel comfortable sharing the uncomfortable. If they are willing to ask or share most anything, that's a good sign. It can create some awkward or tense moments, but it's honestly an indication of a healthy culture when people can share freely and not fear retaliation for honest feedback. Don't get me wrong, there is an appropriate way to do this, and leaders have to provide guardrails for sharing. At the end of the day, engagement can create some great opportunities for feedback.

Surveys—Part One

A useful way to get honest, specific feedback is through surveys. There are several ways you can administer them, and you can be as specific or general as you prefer. I have done surveys where employees put their names on them, but you will most likely get more honest (sometimes brutal) input when they can remain anonymous. Would we like for employees to be willing to be honest while identifying themselves? Of course. Is it likely you will get honest feedback from all employees when we require them to give their names? Not likely. You do have the option of having them identify their current division, unit, or team assignment. This can be helpful in identifying some issues that may be specific to certain areas of your organization.

We do a department-wide survey every summer. You will not get 100 percent participation. You can try to force employees to fill them out, but I don't believe that's a good idea. Forcing employees to share when they don't want to, or feel uncomfortable doing so, will not result in you getting the sincere input you desire. Once the surveys are completed, we move to part two of the process.

Surveys—Part Two

Meet with personnel to go over the survey results. This is a perfect opportunity to go over the input you've received from everyone. You can even send out the results ahead of time, but you have to be careful as you don't want people to be able to identify who said what. You might consider redacting anything that could single someone out or paraphrasing the input in more general terms. Either way, set up survey meetings and talk about the results. I have found this will often spur some really good conversations once people start hearing what others have said. I have also discovered that some employees are willing to expound or go deeper on topics in these meetings, which is very beneficial.

I utilized an innovative idea shared by another chief when I first became a chief. I highly recommend this when someone starts a new leadership position. I sent out a survey to all our employees that asked two questions. What are three things we do well, and what are three things we need to improve on? I let everyone know that I would meet with each employee individually to discuss their input. This first survey was the only time I asked employees to provide their names. I wanted to meet with each one of them specifically and give them an opportunity to provide whatever level of input they felt comfortable sharing. Some surveys literally had one-line answers while others were like essays. My ultimate reason for doing this was two-fold. First, I wanted to quickly send a message that I value employee input. It was important that during one of my first opportunities to engage, I sent a message that they had a voice, and this was their department.

Secondly, I wanted to get a vivid perspective of the good, the bad, and the ugly in our agency. Boy, did I ever. It took me much longer to meet with every employee than I anticipated (they were supposed to be fifteen-minute meetings . . . some lasted five minutes while others lasted as long as an hour). Because I had so much else going on in my new role, it took almost a year to complete all of the meetings, but it was well worth the time. It made me realize we had a lot of work to do on our culture, and it also gave me a chance to provide several small wins in a short timeframe, based on the feedback I received. I also became aware of the fact that our agency had some really sharp and talented people. Another plus related to engagement . . . you truly get a chance to learn about the people in your organization.

Create Teams to Address Specific Topics

Our department has been exploring some different ways we can improve employee retention. As I shared before, we are seeing people getting out of the public safety profession, and we need to work on beefing up employee benefits in an effort to retain good employees. I sent an email to the entire department to share any retention ideas they had up the chain with their supervisors. A lot of ideas were shared, and we created a spreadsheet that captured all of the ideas provided. We then created a team that included supervisors and front-line personnel from several areas in the organization to meet and start discussing the input we received, and how we could create a game plan for making some needed changes. So, we got input on the input. See a theme here?

Whether it's uniforms, vehicles, or equipment, we always try to get several people involved in making decisions. For me, this is a no-brainer because they are the ones that will be wearing the uniforms, driving the vehicles, and using the equipment. They should have some say!

The same concept applies to the benefits example I just shared. Ultimately, these improvements will directly impact them and their families. The employees on these teams have a very important role in representing the people they work alongside. I don't expect everyone to be in complete agreement on most topics, but the goal is to get an accurate consensus on what direction to go in on these types of decisions. Another goal? Help our employees realize they have input on decisions related to *their* department.

Policy and Procedure Input

How do most employees find out about policy changes? Usually, they are *told* what changes have already occurred through some type of inter-office communication. Why not at least give them the opportunity to provide input on proposed new policies, policy adjustments, or other changes in the organization before making those changes final? For example, when a policy change is needed, have a draft created, make that draft available to impacted employees, and ask for comments, questions, or concerns. Oftentimes, we get minimal responses, but employees are given the opportunity for input, and there are times when adjustments are made based on responses from our people. There are instances when good policies are made even better because of employee feedback.

If it's a major change (pursuit policy), you especially want to hear from your people. We don't always make adjustments based on feedback, but there have been several times changes are made because of the input we received. We recently revamped our discipline policy, and we received some great feedback from several employees during meetings and through emailed responses given after employee input was solicited. Again, we made it better, and we created buy-in. Win-win.

Idea Tank

One of my favorite shows on television is Shark Tank. If you are not familiar with the show, five uber-wealthy people listen to pitches made by want-to-be entrepreneurs that are hopeful one of the five business tycoons will invest in their new business idea. Sometimes, the "Sharks" like what they see and will make investment offers. If it's a really good idea, several sharks may compete with each other to try to get a deal. On the other hand, these potential investors may have zero interest in what they are seeing and will, at times, provide some brutal feedback about why they have no interest in investing. Overall, a lot of new products and businesses have been born on Shark Tank because someone very rich invested in a winning idea that ended up making all parties involved a lot of money.

We have created our own version of Shark Tank. If an employee has an idea they would like to see implemented in our department, they are invited to our main conference room and will present their idea to several command staff members. Generally, if the idea meets the mission and we can afford it, we will give it a shot. We have had some amazing ideas that worked really well, and we have had others that simply did not pan out. Either way, it is another avenue employees can use to share ideas on how to make us better, and it also helps them sharpen their presentation skills, which is an additional benefit. Honestly, I would love more ideas shared through our idea tank, but all of our employees know it's an option, whether they choose to take advantage of it or not.

Coffee Conversations

These are basically intentional one-on-one conversations where leaders solicit input from an employee. I have a coffee shop in our city where I like to have these meetings with employees, but these conversations can take place anywhere. As a matter of fact, they don't always have to be planned conversations. You may come across someone in the parking lot, breakroom, hallway, etc., and have an opportunity to have a quick chat with them about a topic you want some input on. At times, I am intentional in meeting with people that may have some expertise in an area, and at other times, I will just randomly sample people on topics of interest. The more I ask, the more quality input I receive, and the more a message is sent that I want to hear from our people.

A QUICK CLOSING THOUGHT

Listening is great, but there has to be an action that follows. I am by no means saying all input and ideas are good or plausible. Leaders also have to be good at saying no sometimes. But if the answer is no all the time, or there is never any follow-up, people will quickly assume that your "desire for input" is nothing more than lip service. When people take the time to provide their ideas and it leads to changes or improvements, make a big deal about it. Let these moments serve as examples of how the organization operates under your leadership. Employee input is not only an option, it's expected.

One of our divisions made a slight adjustment in how we conduct outside training. I won't bore you with the minor details, but the change came from management. Soon after the change was instituted, a front-line supervisor immediately noticed some flaws in the new process. He contacted a major about his concerns. He was right. That major contacted me and let me know that we had made a mistake and needed to change it, which we did. When we shared that we had made a mistake and needed to make another protocol adjustment, we gave a shout-out to this supervisor for running his concern up the chain and ultimately "making it better." I was out of town when all of this happened, but I called him to personally thank him for making us aware of our error. By the way, he felt comfortable reaching out to this particular command staff member because that executive consistently engages with our staff and this employee knew his feedback would be welcomed.

" Time and growth.
Those same basics are
paramount for leaders
developing their people . . .
spending time with them
and helping them grow. **"**

Chapter 7

AN ONGOING DEVELOPMENT

A RECENT ARTICLE in the Harvard Business Review highlighted research done by LinkedIn in 2019. According to the study, 94 percent of the people surveyed stated they would stay in their current job if their employer would invest in them.[13] Basically, that means that people will be invested in where they work if where they work is investing in them. We can excel at attracting quality candidates. Organizations can provide a robust onboarding program for new hires. Many companies are diligent about creating work environments that provide a comfortable, employee-centric atmosphere. Those are all important parts of hiring and retention. However, if we fail to develop them once we get them in the door, we are not providing compelling force leadership that creates value for its employees. We strive to hire and retain employees to make us better. We must be intentional in helping make them better.

Too often, people get into a certain role, get pigeonholed, and become stale and miserable. No change, no development, no opportunities to try something new, and ultimately, no growth. Let's be honest, there are employees that don't want to grow,

---

[13] Anand Chopra-McGowan, "Effective Employee Development Starts with Managers," Harvard Business Review, March 2, 2022, https://hbr.org/2022/03/effective-employee-development-starts-with-managers.

because growing can involve more effort and getting outside of their comfort zone. That's on them. It's our job, as leaders, to provide a path to growth for those that desire it. This should be the expectation, not the exception. If we create a culture that excels in employee development, then those that don't want to be developed and grow will continue to work in a state of status quo and will likely go away at some point.

Remember what we said about not having to have recognized authority to be a leader? Ultimately, that is what development is all about . . . helping create and grow leaders in your organization, regardless of their rank or role.

John Maxwell is another author that is a leadership legend. He has been training leaders for decades. One of his most popular books is *The 21 Irrefutable Laws of Leadership*. The twentieth law in this book is the Law of Explosive Growth. He starts that chapter with, "To add growth, lead followers—to multiply, lead the leaders."[14] Status quo employees typically make up 20 percent of our workforce. According to Maxwell, we can spend 80 percent of our time focusing on that 20 percent of our people if we are not careful.[15] That is not a wise investment of our time. I completely agree with his perspective that we should reallocate that 80 percent of our time and focus on our leaders and those that want to be developed. If we provide tools and opportunities for growth for the men and women that embrace the cultural values we cherish, their influence will expand and impact the overall health of our organizations. We want multiple compelling force leaders—those that add value to *people* with *purpose* and *passion*. If influence is a key to leadership, we must prioritize the development of leaders that intentionally utilize their influence toward the greater good of the organization.

---

[14] John C. Maxwell, *The 21 Irrefutable Laws of Leadership* (Nashville, TN: Thomas Nelson, 2007).

[15] Dave Schoenbeck, "John Maxwell's Leadership Law #20: The Law of Explosive Growth," Dave Schoenbeck, December 23, 2019, https://daveschoenbeck.com/john-maxwells-leadership-law-20-the-law-of-explosive-growth/.

So, from a logistical perspective, how should leadership development take place? One leader can't develop everyone, correct? It would be impossible for Michael Dowling to personally develop the seventy-six thousand employees of Northwell Health. Even the CEO of a small company with only thirty employees would struggle to strategically help his or her influential leaders grow. Every situation has its own unique challenges for leadership, but the best approach is for leaders to focus specifically on those over which they have direct influence. We should be flexible in regard to whom we can help excel in their roles, but there is always wisdom in having a game plan when it comes to growing people and growing organizations. If people occupying a leadership position have men and women that report directly to them, then it would make sense that those are the people they should focus on first.

Imagine a large company president that has five vice presidents he or she works with directly. Those five vice presidents could greatly benefit from the president investing time and resources into their development. Ideally, each one of those vice presidents is being prepared to take his or her leader's position one day. It's an old adage, but it's true that leaders should work toward training their replacements. When there is an expectation that leaders embrace the strategic approach of preparing those that report to them to eventually replace them, this is an excellent indicator of a healthy culture.

The concept of developing others applies to any level of leadership. The CEO and his or her executive managers. The mid-level managers and their front-line supervisors. The front-line supervisors that directly supervise line-level employees. The experienced, line-level employees that have influence over less experienced team members. Leaders in any position can and should engage in the development of those they influence. For me, it's the five executive command staff members that directly report to me. Although I want to be able to develop others on our team in various ways, those five are the ones I should intentionally invest in the most. As you read this and hopefully strategize a development approach for your team, keep your direct reports, or those you directly influence, in mind, as you contemplate how you can add value to these leaders by developing them.

FOUR PHASES OF EMPLOYEE DEVELOPMENT

Engagement: There is a lot that goes into parenting. My kids are grown, and I cannot imagine raising young children in today's world. Today's parents have challenges I never had when it comes to kids—especially as it relates to technology and social media. As our younger kids started getting older, we had to have those conversations about when was the right time to let them have a cell phone.

Now, they are born and come home from the hospital with a phone and an Instagram account. Every generation faces different challenges related to being parents, but I do believe there are two extremely important aspects of parenting that have always existed, regardless of what's going on in the world. Good parents spend quality time with their kids, and they constantly work toward helping them grow into productive adults. Time and growth. Those same basics are paramount for leaders developing their people . . . spending time with them and helping them grow.

The further we get into the 3P Leadership approach, the more we will see the elements of compelling force leadership all intertwining. So much of what we referred to in the last two chapters regarding communication was contingent upon leaders practicing engagement. The same can be said about the correlation between engagement and employee development. You cannot effectively develop people that don't ever see you. Engagement is important at all levels of the organization, but leaders should spend the most time with those they are directly responsible for or have the opportunity to influence the most. Honestly, this will often organically occur because of the necessary interaction between people on teams that work together. There is very little I do in my job that does not involve working with my executive team. However, I should always be intentional in creating opportunities for them to grow beyond just working with them to get the job done. There is a difference between working as a team and working as a team in a manner that benefits team member growth.

To be clear, healthy engagement and micromanaging are not the same. A micromanager will absolutely stifle employee development. When employees are only shown what to do, or told specifically what to do by their bosses, they are missing out on tremendous opportunities for growth and development. A developmental strategy for growth will not be sustained if we don't provide our people the tools to do the job and then let them do it. In today's work environment, we especially want employees that are proactive problem solvers. Even in public safety, where we have lived in a world of reactively responding to calls for service for generations, we need people that are invigorated by meeting challenges and finding the solutions to problems. These are our influential leaders. Our role should be to equip them to do this, and then let them go. Sure, we need to set expectations and provide guardrails. But employees that are game changers—and ultimately leaders—are the ones that proactively figure out how to get the job done. A part of what we do, as leaders, is teach, guide, and instruct. Yet, if that is all we do, employees will be stifled with no opportunities to grow and expand. Remember, we all get better when our people get better. Make sure you engage with your team, but always be careful to not allow that engagement to transition into attempting to do their jobs for them.

Education: One of the ways you can assess an organization's commitment to its people, and specifically employee development, is by looking at how much of its budget is dedicated to education and training. Compelling force leaders understand the importance of providing effective training for their employees, especially those influential men and women that are always looking to grow and improve. Unfortunately, we often see employees get just enough training to work adequately in their current role, and no more. Again, no opportunities to grow, no new experiences, no fresh ideas . . . just coming to work with no hope of change or new challenges. I am getting bored just thinking about it.

I am a big believer in cross-training, or training in a way that helps people move toward their career goals. Now, don't get me wrong. If an employee wants opportunities for training to expand their knowledge base of a job or profession, they should earn that opportunity. Even if there is not a direct correlation between their current role and a training opportunity that focuses on another area of the organization, they can benefit and so can the organization. The more they know, the more they grow, and the more it will show in their work. That's good stuff . . . know plus grow equal show.

Seriously, people with a greater understanding of the inner workings of a company, even if it's outside of their current job description, will likely be better employees. Also, offering training opportunities can be a reward for a job well done.

Imagine you have an employee who truly wants to be a supervisor in your organization. They are consistently demonstrating the leadership characteristics valued by your organization. Why not send them to some leadership training? It can be a reward for a job well done. It will also potentially help prepare them for a future leadership role. It does not guarantee they will ever work in a recognized position of authority, but it certainly improves their chances. Also, it will most likely equip them to be a more effective employee in their current role.

A real example in my world is when a patrol officer expresses their desire to be a detective. When manpower allows, we will send them to our Criminal Investigation Division and let them shadow a detective and learn some of the basics of investigative work. Even when back on patrol, they can utilize some learned investigative techniques they gained during the on-the-job training they received. We also try to send them to classes that are centered around investigations. This also means they are now on the radar of the supervisors in the investigation unit as well. Again, they are being rewarded for doing a good job, they are an even better officer because of the new skills they have developed, and they have an improved chance of fulfilling their goal of becoming a detective one day. Even if that, for some reason, never happens, they know their department has invested in them.

I understand that we all have challenges, and sending people away to training can be difficult, especially when staffing is at a premium. Having people that are cross trained can certainly allow more flexibility. When considering the most effective approach to departmental operations, emphasizing employee education is a must. A healthy culture typically includes ample chances for employees to better themselves through educational opportunities.

Evaluation: Almost all organizations have some type of employee evaluation process. The effectiveness of these tools is another topic for another book, but let's just say we often miss the mark when it comes to providing effective, consistent feedback that can equate to employee growth. *People-oriented leaders don't just evaluate their employees, they provide feedback based on their evaluations that can benefit and develop them.* I am not just talking about rating employees on a scale from one to five using terms and descriptions provided by a human resources evaluation matrix. I am talking about ongoing engagement (there's that word again) that includes honest, constructive feedback.

If we are going to develop leaders, we have to help them see where they need to improve. A tremendous source of growth can be found in people learning from their mistakes. It's easy to give positive feedback, but leaders often struggle with the courageous conversations that should take place involving needed areas of improvement for employees. Why do we struggle so much with these conversations? Because they make us feel uncomfortable. They can be extremely awkward. Emotions can run high. However, who are we making it about when we only consider all of the factors we don't like about giving negative feedback? We are thinking of ourselves. We are making it about us. The key to making sure we have those tough talks is reminding ourselves that we are doing it for the employee. We are doing it for their benefit. This is another tool we can utilize to help them develop. I have found people that truly grasp what's important about growing and leadership want to hear about their shortcomings so they can—you guessed it—*make it better.*

I referred to our unique promotional process earlier. One of the most effective aspects of this process is the feedback provided to those that do not get promoted. Once again, total credit goes to two of our executive leaders that not only had the idea, but actually have the tough job of sharing needed areas of improvement with those that choose to get feedback. The cool part about this is we have several current supervisors that did not get promoted the first, second, and sometimes third time they tried, and yet they took the negative feedback, learned from it, and eventually got promoted. They grew . . . they got better . . . they got promoted. Evaluating our people and sharing feedback based on our evaluation is another path we can provide to help develop our employees.

Emulation: Simply put, you and I should put on display what compelling leadership looks like on a daily basis. We can preach what matters all day long, but if we don't demonstrate it in our own leadership, we fail in credibility, and we miss out on an opportunity for employee development. Going back to my previous parent analogy, part of being a good parent is providing a good example for our kids. It's incredible how much kids pick up on. If kids see it or hear it, they will likely try to repeat the actions or words. For some reason, they especially have a knack for repeating bad behaviors or words. Any parents reading this probably have some stories to tell when it comes to kids picking up on our bad habits.

That same concept applies to leadership and those being led. We should provide an example for those that want to grow as leaders. If we value taking care of our people, they should see us actually displaying that value in our work. If we preach engagement, we should be seen engaging. If we tell our people we value their input, then we should ask for it. If we emphasize the importance of integrity and honesty, then we better practice what we preach. Ultimately, our words and actions must match if we truly want to be effective, influential leaders. Another benefit of consistent modeling is providing an example that can help develop our people. Every day you come to work; remember you are a billboard for what matters most in your organization.

Picture in your mind the greatest leader you have worked for at some point in your career. Of all the jobs you have held, what man or woman is at the top of your effective leaders list? Now, think about two or three attributes of their leadership that led you to ranking them number one on your list . . . maybe it was their integrity, how they took care of their people, led with their boots on the ground, excelled at being a good listener, heavily invested in you, always put others first, or were extremely purpose driven.

Whatever attributes you chose are reflective of what you feel is good leadership. Now, if I went to the people who work with you and know you, would they say you exhibit those same attributes you found effective in your best leader? The answer is most likely yes. One of the ways we become excellent leaders is by *learning* from other excellent leaders. I learned to value people above everything else, partially from working for supervisors that shared the same values. So, as a leader in your organization, you have the opportunity to help your people grow by effectively mirroring superb leadership qualities.

PRACTICAL POINTS

As with so many aspects of quality leadership, intentionality is extremely important. Here are some intentional steps leaders can take to develop employees in their organization:

Career Mapping

Ensure career mapping is a part of the onboarding process for new employees. Make time to sit down and learn about their experience, talents, and interests. Help them see a potential (we never make promises) path to get them where they want to be. Work with them to help them understand expectations and create a game plan for their future.

When we hire new employees, someone from our command staff takes the new team member to lunch to talk about what's next, what our expectations are, our culture, etc. A part of that conversation is talking with them about what their short-term and long-term goals are (knowing, of course, these could change) and providing them some guidance on how to achieve those goals. When we hire people with previous experience, this is especially helpful as they already have a grasp of the positions, units, and divisions that are common in our profession.

Cross-Training

I already provided a couple of examples of this development tool. Once employees have grown comfortable and effective in their assigned roles, they can begin to explore some other areas they can learn from that they may be interested in pursuing. If they are doing a good job and earning new opportunities for growth, start looking for on-the-job and outside educational opportunities. The more they learn from other areas, the more it benefits them and your organization.

Let Them Do Your Job

When possible, let those you are investing in take on the tasks that are a part of your regular responsibilities. Ideally, they learn from watching you do it, and then they learn from actually doing it themselves. Don't forget to evaluate and offer feedback. For instance, let's say there are certain presentations you have to deliver as a part of your job. If it's allowable and prudent, provide someone you are developing an opportunity to make one of those presentations. I often have to present to our government officials. At times, I will have other executive staff members handle one of these presentations. This can certainly be an intimidating task, but it's a great opportunity for growth.

When you are out of the office on vacation or in training, put someone else in charge of your team, unit, division, or department. Send out a notice that he or she is in charge during your absence and let them do what you normally do while you are gone. You don't want to throw them to the wolves and set them up for failure. Make sure and use good judgment regarding when they are ready to take on these growth opportunities.

Leadership Academy

Come up with internal leadership training. You can actually kill two birds with one stone here. You, or someone you bring in, can train the leaders in your organization on how they can be compelling force leaders. You can spend a lot of money on training and speakers, which is great. If the budget is tight, there is a lot of material available online or in leadership books that can help equip you or others in your organization to teach what transformational leadership resembles in a daily work environment. Be sure to use people that are gifted in presenting. If that's not you, that's okay. You want to make sure this training is dynamic and interesting. You can also use this time (the second bird) to emphasize your values or talk about administrative or procedural topics that need to be addressed. There are several ways you can make good use of this time, but the ultimate goal is leadership development.

Leadership Book Group

This is something you can open up to anyone in the organization. Pick a good leadership book and set up monthly meetings at lunch to go through it together. Be intentional about picking a book that you feel reflects what's important in leadership in your organization. Create a few discussion questions and go over them as a group. We normally go through a book in four or five months. We buy them books, and they bring their own lunch for these hour-long gatherings. A great, low-cost way to develop people throughout your organization.

Personality/Strengths Assessments

There are some great tools available to help assess the strengths and passions of your people. Knowing what makes them tick and how they are wired can help you place them in roles and circumstances that will expedite their growth and contentment for their jobs. You don't want to put a behind-the-scenes kind of employee in front of a crowd, leading a seminar. That could actually stunt their growth. Conversely, someone that is more geared toward engagement will thrive and grow in roles that have them working with people versus working alone.

We have used two assessments with our leadership team that I have found very effective. The first is the DISC assessment, which I previously mentioned. This assessment has been around for a while, but I continue to be amazed at how accurately it measures where employees are strong and weak in the areas of *d*ominance, *i*nfluence, *s*teadiness, and *c*ompliance. Please note, there is no wrong outcome. An employee that scores high on dominance will likely grow more and be more fulfilled when leading a team project. At the same time, if I need research and data for a project, I know that my leaders who scored high on compliance will do a great job of getting the details we need to ensure success, and they will benefit from fulfilling their roles.

A new assessment I recently discovered is the Working Genuis, which was developed by one of my favorite authors, Patrick Lencioni. There are six working geniuses: wonder, invention, discernment, galvanizing, enablement, and tenacity.[16] Typically, people have two working geniuses (where they thrive), two working competencies (can get the job done, but not their

---

[16] Patrick Lencioni, "The Six Types of Working Genius," workinggenius.com (The Table Group), https://www.workinggenius.com/.

strongest area), and two working frustrations (roles that result in frustration). For me, my working geniuses are wonder (big picture leadership, wondering how we can make it bigger and better) and galvanizing (effective at rallying people around a project or idea and inspiring them). On the other hand, I would be miserable if you asked me to be creative (invention) and needed me to push others toward completing (tenacity) a task. I encourage you to go to workinggenius.com to learn more about this tool.

PART THREE

3P LEADERSHIP—
PURPOSE

"Even when our schedules and tasks get altered, our purpose should never be altered."

Chapter 8

PURPOSE-DRIVEN LEADERSHIP

I LOVE SPORTS for several reasons. Watching football, basketball, baseball, or any other sport live is truly the greatest reality TV available for viewing. For the players and coaches, the goal is pretty simple: win. The players want to win. The coaches want to win. The fans want to win. That's the goal. That's the purpose. Just win. For coaches, they can talk about creating culture, growing players, and effectively representing their school, community, or city. Those are all noble aspirations. But at the end of the day, their ultimate job is to win games. Typically, coaches that are not able to win don't coach very long. However, one of my favorite sports stories centers around a coach and program that played an entire college football season where the top priority was NOT winning.

It was 1971, and Marshall University was trying to field a football team a year after enduring one of the greatest tragedies the sports world had ever seen. In 1970, almost the entire Marshall football team was killed in a horrific plane crash. Coach Jack Lengyel, who had enjoyed success as a coach at the College of Wooster, located 230 miles north of Marshall, decided to take the head coaching position at Marshall with the purpose of "saving the program." In a recent interview with Images Arizona, he added how his previous mantra of "winning is everything" had completely changed when he stated, "And then I came here

(Marshall). For the first time in my life, maybe for the first time in the history of sports, suddenly it's just not true anymore. At least not here, not now. It doesn't matter if we win or if we lose. It's not even about how we play the game. What matters is that we play the game. That we take the field, that we suit up on Saturdays, and we keep this program alive."[17]

Coach Lengyel had a clear mission that correlated with the unusual circumstances of Marshall University. He had established a purpose for his role as coach, and he created a purpose for his players and coaches. They existed to make sure Marshall University kept a football team on the field, which they did. Mission accomplished. Purpose fulfilled.

Even President Nixon recognized the fulfillment of this unique purpose when he wrote a letter on September 7, 1971, to Coach Lengyel which read, "but whatever the season brings, you have already won your greatest victory by putting the 1971 varsity squad on the field".

I can only imagine how this purpose helped bring some much-needed healing to such a close-knit community that had endured such an unthinkable tragedy.

Leading with Purpose . . . the second P of 3P Leadership. Transformational leaders are purpose-driven leaders. Purpose-driven leaders help create purpose for their people. When we truly lead and work with purpose, our roles, positions, and jobs become bigger than ourselves. One of our greatest opportunities to use our influence as compelling force leaders is to lead our people on a path to being mission-minded. We cannot effectively create purpose for our people if we don't identify and understand what our own purpose is as a leader. In chapter 9, we will dive into leaders creating purpose for their people. For now, let's look at what it means to create purpose for ourselves.

I can't explore the topic of identifying and understanding our purpose as leaders without talking about Simon Sinek's book,

---

[17] Tom Scanlon, "Jack Lengyel: He Is Marshall," Images Arizona, April 23, 2017, https://imagesarizona.com/jack-lengyel-he-is-marshall/.

Start with Why. If you are serious about being a transformational leader, this book is a must-read. I can't do justice to how well Sinek covered the topic of having purpose (knowing your *why*) and how that should impact your role as a leader. If we are going to be compelling force leaders, it is critical to understand the need to see our roles through the prism of purpose.[18] If you think about it, you likely have a *why* or purpose for several areas of your life. As a husband, I should have purpose when it comes to being married to my wonderful wife. If I just haphazardly go through life with no sense of purpose or goals related to how I should faithfully love her, I am probably not going to be a very good husband. The same goes for being a dad. If I am going to be an effective father, I have to be intentional . . . I have to view my role as a father as one that has purpose. The same can be said for any relationship you have in your life. Your purpose can also change. My *why* as a dad is different now, since my kids are grown, versus what it was when we were raising them in our home.

Think about your current job. You had a purpose for taking that job. It may have been as simple as you needed a job to support your family or pay the bills, or you might be like me and feel like your job is a calling. Regardless, you had a *why* for getting into your current profession. Using an employee as an example, which person is more likely to excel in their role and be committed to your organization: the employee whose purpose centers around working eight hours and getting paid, or the employee that comes to work with purpose and feels like what they do matters? Of course, it's the latter and not the former. The same goes for leaders. Those of us that are driven by purpose will be much more effective than bosses that are centered on themselves, their desires, their wants, and their needs. Why you do what you do matters.

Purpose is especially vital when trying to navigate through difficult times. When the pressure is on, we are feeling burned

---

[18] Simon Sinek, *Start with Why: How Great Leaders Inspire Everyone to Take Action* (New York, NY: Penguin Group, 2009).

out, or we are enduring the rough waters that sometimes rock our boat at work, focusing on our purpose can ensure we stay the course. If we lose sight of our mission, or we have no mission, it will not take much to distract us from doing what's important in our role as leaders. When our job is based on our *why*, our focus will remain resolute regardless of the circumstances we encounter.

Part of becoming a certified officer in Georgia is spending a week on emergency driver's training. This makes sense because police officers spend so much time in a patrol car and often find themselves having to drive in high-stress, dangerous situations. One of the areas of training included having to learn how to navigate a vehicle that is skidding out of control. We spent several hours of training in an old Ford Crown Vic with bald tires on a slick skid pad. As the student would drive onto the pad, and upon direction from the instructor in the passenger seat, they intentionally put the vehicle into a skid. We were trained on steering into the skid to help try to maintain control. Our instructors also told us to find a fixed object ahead of us and focus on that object no matter what. The initial natural inclination was to look toward the direction in which you are sliding. After a couple of practice rounds, I was able to locate and focus on an object, even when skidding from side to side. Staying fixed on that object greatly helped me properly navigate the sliding and skidding and eventually regaining control of the vehicle.

That is what purpose provides for us as leaders. Even when we are in chaos and having difficulty gaining control of our circumstances, remaining fixated on our *why* will ensure we stay the course and eventually regain control.

So, what's your purpose when you come to work every day? Why do you do what you do in your role as a leader? I can tell you that it should, in some way, be about your people. Even in my position, where I lead a department that solely exists to serve our community, my *why* starts with our team. Please understand, I am not always successful at fulfilling my purpose, but ultimately

I view my job as adding value to our people first and foremost. As a matter of fact, everything I talk about in this book supports my very reason for leading. It's actually a fairly simplistic strategy, but it's not always simple to execute. If the people that work in our agency experience value in their job and feel like they are working for something bigger than themselves, they are likely going to perform at a higher level. For us, that results in men and women excelling in taking care of our community. For you, that may mean your people are going to excel in taking care of customers, thriving in the area of sales, or producing high-quality products. Regardless of the profession, leaders that have an employee-centric *why* will greatly enhance the chances of creating an environment where people are much more likely to perform at a high level.

It's easy to get sidetracked. Many of us come to work with ideas of doing what matters most, and oftentimes, those plans get derailed within thirty minutes of being in the office. We all understand what it means to put out fires. There are days it feels like that's all I do. As I said before, I am a big believer in creating tasks with the goal of achieving what's important each day. However, I cannot tell you how many times I go to my task list on my phone and change the reminder date to tomorrow or another day on the items that did not get completed. I know most of you can relate. Even when our schedules and tasks get altered, our purpose should never be altered. While we are on the topic, I will use this as an opportunity to challenge you and me both to reexamine our priorities. We often let ourselves get "too busy" to do what's important because we are not prioritizing what's important. I had always felt like I did a fairly good job at time management. That perception of myself changed when I spent the first six months of my current job running around feeling like I was constantly behind and overwhelmed. I was losing control of my calendar because I was losing perspective of what mattered. I still become sidetracked, but I do feel, after making some adjustments, that I have more opportunities to fulfill my mission and ensure I focus on what matters. You have to prioritize what's important and stick to your guns. That may mean practicing more effective delegating, and it may also mean learning to say no.

I remember hearing years ago that your checkbook is an indicator of what matters to you in life. In today's terms, that would mean looking at your online banking and Venmo transactions. Either way, where you spend your money indicates what you prioritize. The same can be said for your calendar. What you spend the most time doing at work is an indicator of what you value most. Or, if it does not reflect what you truly value, then you have allowed your time to be hijacked by other people or projects.

I cannot imagine the difficulties Coach Lengyel faced when trying to build a coaching staff and field a team with nothing but freshmen and transfers from other schools. If you watch the movie *We Are Marshall*, you will get a good idea of the struggles Coach Lengyel faced in taking on this unique leadership role. But he knew his *why* and let that guide everything he did as a coach, which ultimately led to playing a full schedule of games in 1971. By the way, they ended up winning two games, including their first home game! Remember what I said about sports being the best reality TV show you can watch? Marshall winning their first home game that season was a perfect example of that.

PRACTICAL POINTS

Being driven as a leader with purpose is a daily discipline. It is so easy to get sidetracked and lose sight of what matters most. You literally have to work on developing and maintaining a mindset that helps keep what's important in your line of sight every day. Some practical ideas to help ensure this happens:

Remember the Daily Purpose Question in Chapter 2

How can I add value to my people? Get in the habit of asking yourself that question every day you go to work. I try to look at my calendar and task list while establishing specific ways I can accomplish this with what I have planned for the day. Don't forget to look for unplanned opportunities to add value as well. Starting each day with this question at the forefront of your mind will help get you in a purpose-driven mode.

Create a Personal, Job-Related Mission Statement

What is your *why* every day you come to work? There are a lot of resources out there that can help you craft a specific purpose statement, but ultimately it should connect to what drives you when you are at work. What do you value? What does your organization value? What are you passionate about? How can you add value to your people? As you consider these questions, start jotting down some statements and work toward coming up with a simply stated goal of your current role as a leader. The statement should be specific enough to drive your behavior. Remember, whatever personal mission statement you create, it should somehow center around your people.

Matching Missions

Assuming your organization has a mission (if not, see the next chapter), create a work-related mission for yourself that is connected to your organization's mission. Your agency's mission should be about the people it serves. Take a part of that mission and make it connect to a way you can serve your people. For example, JetBlue's mission statement is, "To *inspire* humanity—both in the air and on the ground." If you were CEO of JetBlue, your mission statement could read something like, "To support and *inspire* the people of JetBlue." The first part of Amazon's mission statement is, "To be earth's most *customer-centric company*." As CEO of Amazon (you would really be rich), your purpose statement could start with, "Serving those who serve our customers by being an *employee-centric company . . .*" Our agency's mission statement centers around *"enhancing the quality of life of* those we serve in our community." My mission, or purpose, as Chief, is to *"enhance the quality of life* of those that serve in our organization." That's *why* I come to work every day. I am very confident that if I am successful in fulfilling this mission, our employees will be more content and committed, and that will create a much higher likelihood of them achieving our agency's mission.

Purpose-Driven Development

As you utilize tools to help you grow in leadership, incorporate tools that align with your purpose as a leader. Be intentional in attending training that correlates with what you value. If you desire to be an influential, transformational leader, you probably would not want to attend a class that is led by an autocratic leader. Instead, you would want to ensure you take advantage of educational opportunities that reflect what matters to you most. The same goes for the books you read, the podcasts you listen to, and even the leaders that mentor you. You don't want to invest time in growth opportunities that will create internal conflict, but instead will help you grow and get better at fulfilling your purpose. Actually, if you are not working toward adding tools to your purpose-driven toolbox, you are not really being developed at all.

I have specific podcasts I listen to regularly that I know align with my leadership style. There are certain authors I am drawn to that have leadership values similar to mine. I do understand that there can be value in reading and listening to alternative leadership approaches. Good leaders are always open to good ideas, regardless of the source. However, the values that drive you as a leader should be well-grounded in conviction. If you are vacillating back and forth between high-level approaches to leading others (example: transformational vs. transactional) you have not really determined what your *why* is and probably need to backtrack and start working on identifying what your purpose will be moving forward.

Chapter 9

PURPOSE FOR YOUR PEOPLE

IT WAS MY introductory meeting with our high-level leaders. There were approximately fifteen people in the room, and I was wanting to use our first time together as an opportunity to share my vision for leadership. More than that, I was hoping to hear from them as I was trying to gauge where we were, culture-wise, in our organization. As you can imagine, almost everyone was hesitant to share what they really thought because they had no clue how I would react—especially to anything negative. I knew enough to know things were not good morale-wise in the organization, but, as expected, I was going to have to earn their trust before they would be willing to share with me what they really thought and felt about our leadership team and about our agency in general.

There was one person that had enough gumption to share what he thought was a major issue with our leadership, and with our entire team. That same person still serves on our leadership team today, and I can assure you, he continues to say the things that everyone else is thinking, which I value and appreciate. He basically told me that our team was full of talented and dedicated people. But he said it's as if our team were all on a boat, floating aimlessly, with no sense of direction. That was a pivotal moment for me. It was then that I realized one of my first challenges was going to be to create purpose, or a *why*, for the entire organization. I needed to display a target that we all could stay focused on, regardless of the circumstances.

Purpose-driven leaders understand the importance of purpose from two perspectives. As we discussed in the previous chapter, these leaders are driven by a mission when leading their organization, team, department, etc. They also can grasp the necessity of helping create purpose for their people. Transformational leaders utilize their influence to inspire and motivate their team in a manner that leads to a sense they are working for something bigger than themselves. Two of the four tenets of transformational leadership, idealized influence, and inspirational motivation, are directly tied to creating purpose for our people.

If I went to one of your employees and asked them, why your company or organization exists, what would they say? If they viewed their job as just that, a job, with no bigger picture perspective of *why* where they work exists, that employee would probably formulate some type of response that relates to the services provided, products produced, etc. That is not necessarily a bad thing, but a team full of people that lack the vision or understanding that what they do is meaningful and bigger than just a job will lead to a team that will struggle with growth and innovation and will ultimately lack purpose and vision. How your people view their job and their organization truly matters.

There is an old parable about three bricklayers that has been around for a long time. While I am not certain how accurate the story is, it does center around true historical events and drives home precisely what we are referring to here. Back in 1671, a well-known architect named Christopher Wren observed three bricklayers working on the rebuilding of St. Paul's Cathedral in London, which had been destroyed in a large fire in 1666. Wren observed that one of the bricklayers was crouched, one was half-standing, and one was standing tall on some scaffolding. He went and asked each of them, individually, what they were doing. The crouching worker stated, "I'm a bricklayer. I'm working hard laying bricks to feed my family." The second bricklayer half standing had a different response when he stated, "I'm a builder. I'm building a wall." However, the third bricklayer standing tall proudly stated, "I'm a cathedral builder. I'm building a great cathedral to the Almighty." Not surprisingly, the third bricklayer was the most productive worker and future leader of the group.[19] There is nothing wrong with what the first two workers said, especially the one that wants to feed his family. Nevertheless, as leaders, we should desire to have people working for us that work with purpose like bricklayer number three. One of our roles is to help create that purpose.

The Yale School of Management did a study on the impact of employees having a sense of purpose related to their jobs, and they specifically studied two different groups of hospital cleaners. One of the groups viewed their work as nothing more than a job. The other group did the exact same work but viewed their job as a very important part of the overall care of patients in the hospital. They worked hard to ensure the cleaning products they used did not irritate the patients. But get this . . . they also were intentional in spending more time in the rooms of the patients that had very few visitors, and they made it their mission to be innovative in their cleaning approach while also practicing consistent engagement with the patients, visitors, and staff. Wow! The employees came to work with purpose, and that purpose centered around other people. I love the following statement that came from Tanveer Naseer Leadership, the organization that referenced the Yale research on the hospital cleaners in an article on creating purpose at work:

> This is something that every leader can do today because it's not about changing what our employees do, but helping them to reframe how they view their

---

[19] Jim Baker, "The Story of Three Bricklayers – A Parable About the Power of Purpose," Sacred Structures by Jim Baker, September 10, 2021, https://sacredstructures.org/mission/the-story-of-three-bricklayers-a-parable-about-the-power-of-purpose/.

contributions. It's about helping them to see and understand the context of their contributions because we're paying attention to them [20]

So how do we help create purpose for our people? Here are some ways we can help ensure that happens:

ESTABLISH YOUR ORGANIZATION'S NORTH STAR

We can effectively help create purpose for our people in their roles by establishing a North Star for the organization. Merriam-Webster defines a North Star as "the star of the northern hemisphere toward which the axis of the earth points" When I was in fifth grade, Astronomy magazine was delivered to our house every month. Yes, I was an astronomy nerd. I will not take the time to dazzle you with my deep, intrinsic knowledge of how the universe works, instead I will just point out that our earth points toward the North Star. Polaris is known as the North Star, and basically shines above the north pole and stays in the same general area. Therefore, it is reliable enough to always provide us with the direction of north.[21]

It is the job of leadership to establish an organization's "North Star" The ship full of employees needs to know what direction to go in, no matter how rough the seas may get. The driver on a slick skid pad needs to know what he or she should focus on, no matter how out of control the car may become. Ideally, everyone that comes to work in your organization, on your team, in your unit, etc., has a strong grasp on why the organization, team, or unit exists.

[20] Tanveer Naseer, "Are You Creating Purpose through Your Leadership?," Tanveer Naseer, January 22, 2019, https://tanveernaseer.com/leading-with-purpose-to-bring-out-the-best-in-employees/.

[21] Preston Dyches, "What Is the North Star and How Do You Find It? – NASA Solar System Exploration," NASA (NASA, July 28, 2021), https://solarsystem.nasa.gov/news/1944/what-is-the-north-star-and-how-do-you-find-it/.

When I say exists, I don't just mean the specific job as it relates to the service being provided or the items being produced. No, we have to make it bigger than just a task or job. In the world of policing, the most well-known, basic mission of law enforcement is to protect and serve. That's good. We certainly want to be in the business of protecting people and property as we serve. Serving others in itself is a noble purpose. But leaders in law enforcement need to create a more specific purpose that connects to what their agency values, as well as what matters to their community. For us, a higher quality of life is very important to our citizens, and this is something our city in general works hard at providing. Therefore, our purpose is to help enhance our citizen's quality of life. Is protecting and serving them a big part of that? Absolutely. But there are so many other ways we can achieve that as an agency, and every employee's role is an important part of fulfilling that purpose. This approach advances us toward creating a purpose that equates to the roles of employees being something bigger than themselves, something more than just a job.

Zappos is an online shoe and clothing company based out of Las Vegas, Nevada. They have become known for excelling in creating a healthy culture and being extremely purpose-driven. From strictly a business perspective, Zappos exists to sell clothes and shoes to make money. However, Zappos has created a purpose for its people that is much more than that. Their mission statement, which is known by their employees as their "WOW philosophy, reads, "To deliver the best customer service possible."[22] This is a great example of a culture-driven company creating a purpose for their people that demonstrates their jobs as much more than just the work they do. Their mission is very specific. When you read it, you know customer service is their number one priority. They exist to provide excellent service . . . not just sell shoes or clothes.

Jason Korman, the CEO and founder of Gapingvoid, a company

---

[22] "Zappos Mission, Vision & Values | Comparably."
https://www.comparably.com/companies/zappos/mission.

that specializes in innovative culture design stated, "Vagueness is the enemy. Few purpose statements are explicit enough to drive behavior." He also said, "Culture is the most powerful management system leaders have at their disposal. Purpose is an essential part of building culture as it has the potential to inform behavior at scale."[23] When leaders create purpose for their people, employees have a reason to show up for work excited and on mission. Leaders must establish a North Star, or mission, that clearly defines the purpose of the organization.

PURPOSE ON PAPER

Once a purpose is established, work on creating a statement that anyone can read—especially employees—and easily comprehend why the organization exists. Some companies have mission statements, some have purpose statements, some have vision statements, and some have all three. Whatever you want to call it, every organization needs a statement that explains its *why*.

To keep it simple, I am going to consider purpose and mission the same here. You can apply this in whatever way fits best for your team. There is nothing wrong with having a specific purpose statement, mission statement, and vision statement. In our agency, we have a mission statement that is supported by our values. For us, our mission is our purpose. Once your purpose is established you can support your purpose with values, fundamentals, and other actionable descriptions of how the purpose should be fulfilled.

If you already have a purpose or mission statement, does it provide clarity that drives employee behavior and establishes customer expectations? I have found that in public safety, most employees don't have a clue about their agency's mission statement. Often, the only time they learn it is so they can recite it during a promotional

---

[23] Marcel Schwants, "5 Leaders Share Their No. 1 Tip for Building (and Sustaining) a Purpose-Driven Business," Inc., August 13, 2020, https://www.inc.com/marcel-schwantes/how-to-build-purpose-driven-business.html.

interview. I have also found that a lot of agencies have very long, drawn-out mission statements. Mission statements can often be a word salad that provides no actionable clarity to team members about their team's purpose. If an established mission statement exists, you may need to look at tweaking it, redeveloping it, or throwing it out and starting over. If you are starting from scratch, or working on updating an existing purpose statement, this can serve as a great opportunity to allow others on your team to contribute their ideas and input to the mission statement development process. It's your job, as a leader, to establish the *why*, but there is great value in having your team be a part of constructing the purpose and establishing clear and concise direction that will inspire employees to engage in purpose-driven behavior.

WHAT PURPOSE LOOKS LIKE

Once we create purpose for our people, we have to be able to give them clear indicators of what it resembles to actually carry out that purpose. Many organizations establish values to provide this clarity. However, when the values are nothing more than terms like "integrity," or "service above all," there is a failure to provide explicit, purpose-driven behaviors for employees. If the purpose is to drive employee behavior, we have to help them see how that behavior looks. Very important . . . values must be actionable and should support the mission. Going back to Zappos, that's exactly what they did. They created 10 values that they describe as "a way of life". They believe these actionable values are the foundation for fulfilling the mission.

- Deliver WOW Through Service
- Embrace and Drive Change
- Create Fun and a Little Weirdness
- Be Adventurous, Creative, and Open Minded
- Pursue Growth and Learning
- Build Open and Honest Relationships With Communication

- Build a Positive Team and Family Spirit
- Do More With Less
- Be Passionate and Determined
- Be Humble[24]

You can clearly see where their purpose is supported by their values. Establishing actionable values can also be a team-driven exercise that can help create buy-in from your employees. Create a team of formal and informal leaders that reflect what matters and are already purpose driven. If you can get your influential people on board with the mission and values, you will have much more success integrating that mission and those values into your agency, team, or division. Also, all of this is crucial in building a healthy culture where employees are engaged—engaged in something bigger than themselves.

So, we have established the need to create a purpose and provide a direction (North Star) for our organizations. We have demonstrated the need to put that purpose in writing in a manner that creates clarity and helps drive employee behavior and performance. Once we have done that, we then need to establish actionable values that demonstrate purpose-driven behavior. After these crucial steps have been taken, there are a few other actions we can take to ensure our purpose continues to become a part of our DNA.

Purposeful Decision-Making: This should go without saying, but as a leader who preaches purpose, you must also practice it. Once your team has an understanding of the team's purpose, your leadership has to reflect that purpose. Earlier, we talked about one of the ways we can develop our people is by emulating how compelling force leadership should look. We need to be the best example of people-centric leadership, and we also need to be the best example of working with organizational purpose

---

[24] "What We Live By." *What We Live By | Zappos.com*, 3 Dec. 2019, https://www.zappos.com/about/what-we-live-by.

by carrying out organizational values. As you are in the process of making decisions, a key part of your process should be determining what is the best option regarding fulfilling your team's purpose. If I emphasize the purpose of quality of life to our people, then make a decision that could lessen the quality of life of our community, I have failed to fulfill our purpose and have lost credibility as a "purpose-driven" leader.

A great example of this comes from CVS Pharmacy. Their publicized purpose is, "We help people with their health wherever and whenever they need us. And we do it with heart. Because our passion is our purpose: Bringing our heart to every moment of your health." Makes sense, right? A pharmacy has a purpose that centers around the health of its customers. However, back in 2014, the leadership of CVS realized they were not fulfilling that purpose by selling two billion dollars' worth of tobacco and tobacco-related products. The decision to sell cigarettes did NOT reflect their *why*, and that led to CEO Larry Melo announcing, in September 2014, they would no longer sell any tobacco-related products. Melo later stated, "But that decision became an important foundational moment and a foundational decision for our company as we were on this journey of becoming more of a health care company."[25] Leaders should lead the way in creating a purpose for their people, and leaders should lead the way in demonstrating what carrying out that purpose resembles.

PURPOSEFUL PROMOTIONS

There are several considerations that should factor into who you promote into recognized leadership positions. One of those factors must be promoting purpose-driven employees that are clearly on board with the mission of the organization. As I previously stated, one of our goals when making promotions is to

---

[25] Nathan Bomey, "How Quitting Tobacco Reshaped CVS: Q&A with CEO Larry Merlo," USA Today (Gannett Satellite Information Network, September 4, 2019), https://www.usatoday.com/story/money/2019/09/03/cvs-pharmacy-tobacco-sales-ceo-larry-merlo/2151148001/.

promote employees already demonstrating leadership acumen. These "leaders without rank" are the men and women that have bought into our agency's mission and come to work every day attempting to carry out that mission. One of the difficulties I have observed regarding building a healthy culture is how lengthy that process can take to materialize. One of the reasons it can be such a timely process is that we often find ourselves with recognized leaders that have occupied their positions for a while and don't care about executing the mission. This is especially the case if you inherit a team that has had inadequate leadership in place long before you arrived. So, when you have opportunities to promote new people, you have to make sure you get it right as far as building your leadership team. A key component of creating a healthy culture is having purpose-driven people in decision-making roles. You and your leadership team will ideally be on the same mission-minded page. However, it can take some time and heartache to get there. Promote the right people.

PURPOSEFUL PLANNING

Hopefully you and your team have embraced the importance of planning. If you don't practice strategic planning, you need to start. When I started my current role, there was no strategic plan in place. Now, every fall, we plan for the next year, and the next several years. It's honestly still a work in progress, and we continue to tweak how we execute it, but, this is another way we can intentionally implement methods of meeting our mission. For every plan we put into place, we should be able to see somewhat of a nexus of how the execution of the goals associated with those plans ensures we are meeting our mission.

PURPOSEFUL HIRING

We all desire to hire people that are going to eventually be experts at their jobs. We also need to hire people that are going to fit our culture and be on board with carrying out our purpose.

Whatever your hiring process is, you need to try to determine if candidates for hire are a good fit for what you are striving to accomplish as an organization. If they are not, they will likely never embrace your team's *why*, which will create frustration for them, and for you. Hiring new people is almost always a gamble. We need to be sure we are asking the right questions, and utilizing hiring mechanisms that demonstrate new hires are not only going to be proficient in the technical aspects of the job, but are also going to be excited about the mission of your organization. You cannot accomplish this unless you have a clearly defined purpose. Trust me, I get it. This is not easy, especially when staffing is a major issue. Yet, it's extremely important that we always emphasize hiring the right people for our team.

PRACTICAL POINTS

The following practical points directly correlate with the purpose-driven categories given throughout this chapter. As always, I want you to be able to walk away with some practical steps you can implement with your team, regardless of where your organization finds itself culture-wise. I can tell you, the process of creating purpose for your people takes time, especially if it's a new concept. Honestly, as in so many other areas of leadership, it's an infinite game. There is never going to be a point where you feel like you have reached the pinnacle of leading a completely healthy culture with a crystal clear mission. It's a tough reality sometimes, but as long as you keep climbing the mountain, great things can happen.

Establishing Your North Star

I have already referred to Sinek's *Start with Why* several times. So, let me make it easy . . . read *Start with Why*, and his next book, *Find Your Why*. As a matter of fact, have your leadership do the same thing. Go through these books together. This will help you all move in the direction of coming to a consensus on what should be driving your team.

An article by Hubert Joly in Harvard Business Review (a great leadership resource) called Creating a Meaningful Corporate Purpose[26] provided several steps for creating an organizational purpose. The first consideration he listed for defining a team's purpose is especially helpful in identifying what your organization's purpose should be. He advised looking for purpose by addressing four specific factors:

1) What the world needs. When you look at your "world," what needs do they have that your organization can help meet?

2) What people at the company are passionate about. What gets your people excited about coming to work? Where do they desire to make a difference?

3) What the company is uniquely good at accomplishing. What skills, abilities, and talents do your team possess that can address specific needs in your "world"? What can your team do that others can't?

4) How the company can create economic value. If your organization is for profit, this is especially crucial. For nonprofit organizations like ours, you can alter this to examine what type of community-related values can be created by your team. The "how can I add value" question can be applied to the community or groups that you are serving.

Purpose on Paper

This should only be done once you have a clear understanding of what your purpose is and what you value as an organization. Ultimately, you are trying to answer the question, "why do we

---

[26] Hubert Joly, "Creating a Meaningful Corporate Purpose," Harvard Business Review, April 4, 2022, https://hbr.org/2021/10/creating-a-meaningful-corporate-purpose.

exist?" or "why do we do what we do?" What you need to avoid is trying to create a mission statement when you have no clear answer to those questions. If you are not sure of your purpose, don't create a vague mission statement that will serve no value for your team.

There are a lot of resources out there that can guide you in developing a specific mission or purpose statement that will help drive employee behavior. Once you have identified your *why* in general, research other organizational mission statements. There are a ton of examples on the internet that you can easily find. This can help spur some creativity when creating your own. I am by no means saying copy another mission statement word for word, but taking the time to research on the internet several mission statement examples can be helpful during the process.

As you and your team begin to try to build a mission statement, focus on what you value, what will help inspire your employees, what is reasonably attainable, and what is identifiable. As I stated before, the heart of our mission statement is enhancing the quality of life in our community. Our mission fits those four *what* statements:

1) **What We Value:** serving and taking care of our community.
2) **What Will Inspire Our Employees:** we can sell our employees on how meaningful and impactful it can be to serve others.
3) **What is Reasonably Attainable:** Going beyond protecting and serving and viewing our jobs as problem solvers is very attainable with a little extra time and attention given to our citizens.
4) **What is Identifiable:** We can point to what it resembles to go above and beyond the expectations of public safety service and to the next level of enhancing the quality of life of those we serve.

What Purpose Looks Like

It is extremely important to create actionable values. Once you have become mission-minded, you can articulate values that support fulfilling that mission. I gave you some good examples of actionable values from Zappos. Ideally, what you value in your organization's culture will correlate with your mission.

I recently read a book that has changed my perspective on this topic. It has not lessened the importance of actionable values, but instead, it challenged me as a leader to lead our team in identifying fundamentals that reflect what matters in our culture. Many of those fundamentals are tied to actionable values. The book, *Culture by Design* is written by David J. Friedman, and is an excellent resource for defining what matters in your organization, which also can impact how you operate as a purpose-driven organization. You want to talk about practical? The subtitle is *8 Simple Steps to Drive Better Individual and Organizational Performance*.

I'll give you one example of a fundamental we already had in place, and one that was given as an example in Friedman's book[27]:

Make It Better

This was a phrase we started to apply to every area in our agency several years ago. Even if we are doing well in an area, we should always strive to "make it better." At the time we started using it, I had no idea that it was an actionable fundamental. It was something leadership identified as important, and something we wanted all of our employees to strive to achieve internally and externally. Can that contribute to healthy culture? Yes. Does that support our mission? Yes. If we go on calls in our community with the idea that we will try to "make it better" for a citizen's current circumstances, that will result in mission accomplished.

---

[27] David J. Friedman, *Culture by Design: 8 Simple Steps to Drive Better Individual and Organizational Performance* (United States: High Performing Culture, LLC, 2018).

Blameless Problem Solving

As soon as I read this example in Friedman's book, I knew we would also adopt this as a fundamental in our agency. We often respond to problems in our community that were self-created problems. It's easy for people in our profession to get frustrated when responding to calls that could have easily been prevented. But if we adopt the fundamental of "blameless problem solving," we won't focus on what caused the problem, but instead, focus on helping our citizens solve that problem, which totally supports our mission.

Purposeful Decision-Making

From a practical standpoint, it's pretty simple. As you ponder all of the considerations for a decision, does the change, new initiative, adjustment, or overhaul you are considering support the organizational mission? If there is a struggle to connect the choice you want to make with your *why*, it's probably the wrong choice. Our purpose should be a primary part of the decisions we make.

Purposeful Promotions

We want to promote leaders into leadership positions. One of the strongest indicators of leadership is working with purpose—working with an understanding that you are doing something that is bigger than yourself. During an interview, Simon Sinek was asked to identify a couple of consistent traits he had observed while spending time with accomplished leaders. His response? They were teachable and humble. I have found that to be so true. I think the humility characteristic is especially crucial when considering promoting someone into a new leadership position. Humility . . . selflessness . . . an "it's not about me" perspective will most likely equate to a leader who is more about the organization than him or herself.

You and your team (remember the importance I discussed

earlier in getting people that work with promotional candidates involved—especially people that understand the purpose of the organization) should look for certain characteristics when promoting that parallel purpose-driven leadership. Here are some to look for:

- **Engagement:** They engage with their peers, subordinates, and supervisors.
- **Make us better:** They demonstrate a proactive approach to making our team better.
- **Character:** They demonstrate important characteristics consistently.
- **Competence:** They are good at what they do.
- **Selfless:** They put others above themselves.
- **Ownership:** They take ownership of their area of responsibility. When something needs to get done or fixed, they don't wait on others to do it, they take care of it.
- **Team Player:** It's a little cliché, but it is still very important. Good, purpose-driven, transformational leaders are team-oriented.

Purposeful Hiring

When interviewing candidates for a specific job, you have to try to determine if they have the skills to do the job. This is a given. It's also important to try to determine if they are a good fit for your culture. Do their values align with your department's values? Beyond doing your homework on their background, checking references, and talking with previous employers, you want to be sure you ask questions that are cultural and purpose driven. Again, numerous resources out there can assist you with creating hiring questions that will connect with your organization's *why*. Hiring people is always a gamble, but you want to do all you can to try to determine upfront if the candidate's purpose and values align with your department's purpose and values.

Here are some examples:

- What is drawing you to this profession, and more specifically, what is drawing you to our organization?
- What gets you excited about coming to work?
- What is your impression of our organization's culture?
- What are your long-term career goals?
- Describe the best supervisor you have ever worked with or for in your career. What characteristics of his or her leadership mattered to you the most?
- Regarding the job you are applying for, what do you believe makes a (name of job) successful?
- Tell about a time you had a conflict with a colleague at work? How did you handle that conflict?
- Describe a time you were really proud of the work you provided in a previous job (if they are really young with little or no job experience, you can generalize this more to school, sports, family, etc.).
- How do you see your personal values aligning with the job you are applying for?
- Our organizational values are _____. Which one of the values resonates with you the most and why?
- Our mission statement states the following: _____. How can you contribute to helping our organization meet that mission?

"You can have all of the talent possible on one team, but if you are not playing as a team with purpose, success becomes much more difficult to achieve."

Chapter 10

PROMOTING YOUR PURPOSE

ONE OF THE greatest athletic teams ever assembled was the 1992 United States Olympic basketball team. Known as the Dream Team, they completely dominated every country they played in Barcelona, Spain, winning every game by an average of 43.8 points. The team was composed of players like Michael Jordon (still the best player to ever play the game), Larry Bird, Charles Barkley, and Magic Johnson—just to name a few. This was the first time professional athletes were allowed to compete in the Olympics. Moving forward, any American team comprised of NBA players and top collegiate players should have dominated all Olympic and other international competitions. Based on talent alone, no matter their opponent, victory should have always been the outcome. Conversely, that dominance began to wane over time. Why? Because their sense of purpose began to fade.[28]

By the 2000 Olympics, the margin of victory had been cut in half, and by 2002, they finished six and three, and in sixth place, in the FIBA World Championships. In the 2004 Olympics, they placed third, winning the bronze medal. Team USA was still fielding the most talented players in the world, yet they were no

---

[28] Don Yaeger, "Chapter 1: Great Teams Understand Their 'Why,'" in *Great Teams: 16 Things High-Performing Organizations Do Differently* (Nashville, TN: W Publishing Group, an imprint of Thomas Nelson, 2016).

longer winning at will. They were losing games they had no business losing because they had lost their purpose. A team that once played with patriotic purpose was now doing nothing more than playing a game.

You can have all of the talent possible on one team, but if you are not playing as a team with purpose, success becomes much more difficult to achieve.

In 2005, the new managing director, Jerry Colangelo, made it his mission to bring the patriotic purpose back to the Dream Team. He knew he had to find a purpose-driven coach that would focus on connecting the team to its mission. He needed a coach that could consistently promote purpose with his players, and he found that person in Duke coach Mike Krzyzewski. Coach Krzyzewski was a West Point graduate and Army veteran. He believed what Colangelo believed, the issue was not a talent problem, it was a culture problem. Krzyzewski made it his mission to reconnect his players with the patriotic purpose of Team USA. In order to fulfill that mission, Krzyzewski knew he had to help his players "feel" their purpose. Not just tell them, not just show them, but create opportunities for them to experience their purpose.[29]

As a veteran, coach Krzyzewski was able to form partnerships with the military so players could truly grasp the importance of representing their country. He was very intentional in creating numerous experiences with the military. Of all the experiences he created, my favorite involved a field trip to Arlington Cemetery. For those of you that have been there, you know there are truly no words to describe the powerful yet somber view of thousands of white headstones memorializing soldiers who paid the ultimate price for our freedom. While there, Krzyzewski took the players to Section 60, where many of the most recent soldiers that had been killed in the line of duty were buried.

During their visit, they came across a soldier that was there honoring one of his brothers who had died while serving his

---

[29] Yaeger, *Great Teams.*

country. The soldier ended up speaking for a few minutes to the entire team, and his spontaneous words were very moving and inspirational. Once he walked away, coach Krzyzewski told his players, "That is why we came here — to feel our country."[30] This was just one of many examples of Krzyzewski intentionally connecting the players with a purpose that was bigger than themselves. They weren't just playing games with the goal of outscoring their opponent. No, it was much bigger than that. They were playing for that "USA" printed on the front of their jerseys. There were representing the United States of America.

Once again, we are seeing tenets of 3P Leadership building upon one another. One of the key components of adding value to *people* is effective communication up and down the chain. Well, providing clarity to our *people* about our *purpose* is a crucial role of leadership, and that happens through effective communication. Patrick Lencioni has referred to the CEO being the CRO — Chief Reminding Officer, in his writing and on his podcasts. In other words, leaders are responsible for reminding their people of what matters most. As you read earlier, it's paramount that compelling force leaders remind their people of their value. But as we continue to talk about the necessity of creating purpose for our people, we have to focus on the importance of leaders consistently and effectively keeping that purpose in front of his or her employees. That's exactly what coach Krzyzewski did with his Team USA players. He was very intentional in connecting his players with the team's purpose. Once we have established why we exist and what we value, we have to create and maintain a strong connection between the team and what matters most.

So, how do we keep the mission on the radar of all the people in our organization? Let me start by saying you can never remind people enough. A lot of research has been done on how many times someone must hear something before they truly absorb it. Often, the number seven has been identified as the number of times it takes for a person to be able to recall or be impacted by a

---

[30] Yaeger, *Great Teams.*

message. However, leaders don't need to hang their hats on communicating important messages a prescribed number of times. We cannot just assume that once we hit a magic number, we no longer have to concern ourselves with the messaging of our purpose and values. Actually, it's a never-ending process. Part of our mission must be to always communicate the organization's mission to our team.

It sounds a little crazy, but you almost want your people to get sick of hearing you communicate what matters most. You know you are being an effective communicator of purpose when employees come to a point of just assuming you are somehow going to interject departmental purpose into your routine messaging. If you are not familiar with the story of how Alan Mullaly turned Ford around, it's worth taking the time to read about it. It's a great story of a compelling force leader who saved a huge corporation from bankruptcy. One of Mullaly's first tasks as CEO was to create a simple, four-point plan. Mullaly began every meeting by going over his plan. He created wallet cards with the plan in writing for all Ford employees. He talked about it non-stop. Bryce Hoffman, the author who wrote about Mullaly's great work at Ford once said of Mullaly's four points, "After six months, those of us who followed the company had gotten sick of hearing about them."[31] That's exactly what you want!

Before we get into the different ways you can consistently communicate the mission, please understand that your people won't buy into it if they don't believe you are sold on it as well. The next section centers on the importance of passionate leadership. If you don't get excited about the mission, neither will your people. I took a required health class in high school, and my teacher was the baseball coach. Now, no offense to him, but baseball was his passion, not teaching health to a bunch of high

---

[31] Sean Conner, "Say It 7 Times: The Art of Overcommunication," Medium (Unexpected Leadership, October 4, 2018), https://medium.com/unexpected-leadership/say-it-7-times-the-art-of-overcommunication-5d019b2c33d4.

school freshmen. Therefore, the class felt like we were all—including the teacher—just doing what we all had to do to get through it. Basically, we just needed to check the box by fulfilling a requirement. Again, not his fault. I actually played for him as a baseball player, and I can assure you, he was passionate about coaching. When selling purpose to our team, we have to be sold on it ourselves.

One other important point. I am not pollyannish about this. No matter how well you do at leading your organization in being mission-minded, not everyone will get on board. I wish there was a magical formula that would equate to every employee coming to work every day with great purpose. If you figure that formula out, you need to write a book about it! Like almost everything we do in leadership, even when we do it correctly, it's not necessarily going to resonate with everyone. However, if you set the tone and make it clear that being a mission-minded organization is paramount, then you are creating expectations for your employees. At the end of the day, it's up to them whether they meet those expectations, but leaders should provide a clear *why* that will lead to setting employees up for success. The response of a small group of employees should not dictate the decisions made by the leaders. What I can tell you from personal experience is that striving to be a purpose-driven organization greatly impacts the majority of employees, and that's what compelling force leadership is ultimately all about.

With that said, let's look at some avenues we, as leaders, can intentionally utilize to ensure we are constantly connecting our people to the mission.

MISSION-MINDED LANGUAGE

We all have different styles of communication. According to the Office Dynamics International Communication assessment, I am very red (which matches my high "D" on the DISC). Basically, this means that my style of communicating is short, sweet, and to the point. Whether you are a leader that is red like me, or your communication style centers around wanting details, wanting to feel valued, or wanting to feel involved, we must be intentional in speaking about our organizational purpose. What words or phrases connect with your mission? Try to use those words or phrases when communicating verbally or in writing. When you are mission-minded, you may be surprised how many opportunities you have to insert what's important in your culture into your communication.

We have already spent a good bit of time on the importance of engagement. Once again, intentional and opportunistic engagement can create opportunities for us to utilize our influence, and in this case, influence our people toward being purpose driven. We don't want to create an impression that our goal every time we open our mouth is to talk purpose. That will ultimately cause people to tune us out as soon as our conversation morphs into work mode. However, if we are purpose minded when speaking to groups, or in one-on-one conversations, we will see opportunities to appropriately emphasize our purpose or values. Intentional, compelling force leaders take advantage of opportunities to highlight their why. Ideally, it becomes a natural part of our vocabulary without offsetting the other benefits that are gained from engaging with our team. I previously shared about the leader I worked with that made it a habit to ask people, "Is there anything I can do for you?" People knew he was being sincere, but at the same time, he was verbalizing our leadership purpose of adding value to others. Even though he is no longer a part of our team, you will often hear our leaders ask the same question, or at least something very similar. It's a sincere question that reflects our quality-of-life mission, and it demonstrates adherence to our purpose.

When you are communicating about a new initiative in your strategic plan, why not briefly touch on how that new initiative connects with the department's mission? If your mission somehow is centered around a high level of customer service, when you create a new service protocol, be sure and demonstrate how that new protocol is supporting the mission of providing excellent customer service. In our department, when we make changes or initiate something new, we should be able to connect it to enhancing the quality of life of those we serve. Earlier, I talked about the importance of explaining the reasoning behind decisions being made. When you communicate change, explain why the change is taking place. Also, add to that how the change connects to the organization's purpose. Basically, you have a three-step process you can utilize for almost all communication of changes or new initiatives, which can help ensure you are communicating effectively:

COMPELLING FORCE COMMUNICATION

1) Clearly articulate the change or new initiative.
2) Provide the reason for the change or new initiative.
3) Connect the change or new initiative with the mission of the organization.

TELL ME A STORY

Utilizing stories is a proven tool for effective communication. Anytime you can help the receiver of information connect through a memorable story, there is a greater likelihood that what's being communicated will resonate with whoever is listening or reading. I love what Vanessa Boris said about the power of storytelling in an article she wrote in the Harvard Business Review:

> Telling stories is one of the most powerful means that leaders have to influence, teach, and inspire. What makes storytelling so effective for learning? For starters, storytelling forges connections among people, and between people and ideas. Stories convey the culture, history, and values that unite people. When

it comes to our countries, our communities, and our families, we understand intuitively that the stories we hold in common are an important part of the ties that bind.[32]

Influence, inspiration, forging connections among and between people and ideas—all of that is at the heart of leadership and communication! Once we find out our *why* as an organization, we should do everything we can to connect our people to that purpose, and telling stories is an excellent way of achieving that. I especially love telling stories about our people and how they have demonstrated our mission. Your employees will be more tuned into stories about their coworkers. Plus, anytime you point out how an employee is meeting the mission, you are not only communicating the mission, you are also adding value to that employee by focusing the spotlight on them and their important work. Win-win!

I love watching movies, but I especially love watching movies based on true stories. Anytime I see a movie that is supposedly derived from real-life events, I immediately research to see how accurately the movie portrayed those events. Often, several liberties are taken by the movie makers to make it more interesting to a wide variety of audiences. For me, I am more inspired by the stuff that really happened. When you watch a movie like *The Pursuit of Happyness*, *A Beautiful Mind*, or *Apollo 13*, how can you not walk away inspired? Why? Because they are amazing stories about people—people we can relate to and appreciate. Don't get me wrong, I love a good *Avengers* movie or intense espionage drama (Jason Bourne was the man!). Nonetheless, those kinds of movies never connect with me at a deep level because they are

---

[32] Vanessa Boris, "What Makes Storytelling so Effective for Learning?," Harvard Business Publishing (Vanessa Boris /wp-content/uploads/2018/12/HBPubCorpLearn_wide_crimson.svg, February 4, 2019), https://www.harvardbusiness.org/what-makes-storytelling-so-effective-for-learning/.

not true. There is something about a true story, with real people, that resonates at a more meaningful level. The same goes for communicating what matters to our people. Abstract information is a form of communication. But when you communicate with your people at a deeper level by giving them examples of what living your purpose at work resembles, you are helping to create a better, purpose-driven team. You have stories that can exemplify your purpose. Tell them.

RECOGNIZING MISSION ACCOMPLISHED

Hopefully, celebrating good work performed by employees in your organization is the norm. We should always make a point of celebrating excellence, as that is certainly another avenue for adding value to our people. But are you celebrating employees who demonstrate your purpose being carried out? If not, you are missing a good opportunity to drive home the message of the mission. Whatever recognition for a job well done you are presenting or sharing is a golden opportunity to connect the employee's good work to the organizational *why*. Whether it's the top sales executive for the month, an employee who got very positive feedback from a consumer, or a firefighter that performed CPR and saved someone's life, there is a strong likelihood that those well-deserved kudos can also be used as stories of your people demonstrating organizational purpose. Remember the power of stories? Well, when men and women on our teams demonstrate the mission, those are stories worth telling.

Let me take it even further. What about those moments when an employee may be simply "doing their job" but go above and beyond the call of duty in demonstrating the mission being carried out? Should you recognize those moments? You bet you should. Celebrate the excellent work, but also honor those purpose-driven moments that may not necessarily rise to the level of a departmental award but still deserve to be recognized. In other words, be intentional in recognizing specific actions where employees showed their connection to your organization's mission.

A prime example is the story I shared earlier about the hospital cleaners. Is it important they do a great job of keeping the hospital clean? Of course. That's what they are supposed to do, and they should be recognized for really caring about how well they do their job. Nevertheless, is there value in recognizing their purpose-driven behavior that is not necessarily in their job description . . . like intentionally spending extra time in the rooms of patients with no family? Yes! That kind of selflessness and care should be celebrated. When their story is told, it not only adds value to them by recognizing their extra care for the patients, but it can reinforce commitment to the mission.

We created a way to recognize employees in our agency that specifically demonstrated our agency's purpose (see practical points below). One of the first times we recognized some of our employees for being purpose driven was related to a call involving a four-year-old girl that had been kidnapped. She lived in Oklahoma with her mother, and her estranged father took her from their home and somehow ended up in our city. Our officers eventually found the little girl and arrested the father. Now, the typical protocol would have been to call Family Services and have them pick up the child. This solution would have forced the mother to drive all the way to Atlanta to pick up her daughter. Since all this took place in the middle of the night, a couple of our officers had an alternate idea. Not wanting this frantic mother to have to drive all the way to Atlanta, they asked if they could take the child and drive her to a meeting point at a location that was halfway between Atlanta and where the mother lived in Oklahoma. They determined that the Memphis, Tennessee, area would be a good location.

The officers asked their supervisors for permission to carry out their plan, and the watch commander then called me to ask for the permission on their behalf. I told them I was fine with it as long as Family Services signed off on it, which they did. So, these two officers, who already received a pat on the back for doing an excellent job of locating her, could have easily handed the little girl to Family Services. Instead, they went on the journey to Memphis where they eventually met a very grateful mother. What an amazing story! Shortly after the event, I recognized these officers for their commitment to reuniting an extremely grateful mother with her daughter.

Funny side note, one of the officers is a huge guy. He is a mountain of a man with a very deep voice. I asked him what in the world they did to entertain the little girl for so many hours. His response? "We sang *Wheels on the Bus Go Round and Round* over and over again." An even better ending to a fantastic story!

MISSION ON DISPLAY

Wherever you can post or display your mission/purpose, values, etc., do it. Several years ago, we sent four members of our leadership team to spend the day at Southwest Airlines' headquarters for a Culture Connection event. One of their key takeaways from the trip was how well Southwest displayed what matters to their organization throughout their headquarters. When they walked through their building, they saw their purpose and values everywhere they looked. Ideally, your employees actually see your posted purpose every day they come to work. You can keep it simple, or you can get creative, but make it your goal to clearly communicate the mission of your organization in a manner that anyone walking into your building will have no doubt regarding what's important to your team.

DEBRIEFS

In the world of public safety, we will often debrief major incidents. We have gone so far as encouraging our patrol shifts to conduct a debrief of an incident they responded to on their last shift during their roll calls. Sometimes, it takes just a few minutes, and sometimes it can be much more involved. The purpose of a debrief is to examine a call, talk about what the team did well, and what improvements can be made the next time. This falls in line with the goal of always trying to "make it better." These debriefs also create an opportunity to discuss how the mission was met, or next time, how we can do a better job of meeting the mission. Whatever your version of a debrief is in your profession, use that as a time to examine if the mission was met, and how your team can be even more mission intentional the next time.

WELCOME TO OUR MISSION

It's vital that new hires hear about the mission immediately. They need to sense that the mission statement on the wall is more than just words, it's a purpose that drives employee performance. Emphasize the mission in the interview. Emphasize the mission in their orientation. Emphasize the mission during new employee training. New employees should be able to quickly ascertain what matters most to their new work team.

PRACTICAL POINTS

Once again, let's look at some practical ideas associated with each of the categories of creating purpose that we have explored:

Mission-Minded Language

What words directly connect with your organizational mission? What words directly connect with the values that support that mission? Create a small list of words and phrases and start plugging those words into your communication on a consistent basis. Our purpose words and phrases are "quality of life," "excellence with integrity," "courageous spirit," "selfless service," "add value to our people," and "make it better." Whatever words or phrases you identify as mission critical for your team, department, or organization, your people should be accustomed to hearing or reading those words or phrases in your communication. If you are introducing a new mission or values, send out something each week talking about your purpose and attach a story of someone carrying out that purpose. You can send a weekly "Our purpose," "Our mission," or "Our *why*" email every week. As I mentioned before, there are some great apps that can also help you be creative with this.

Previously, I mentioned the book Culture by Design. I highly recommend this book for culture-oriented leaders for several reasons. One of those reasons is the focus on fundamentals. These fundamentals are statements that directly reflect our purpose and values. We are currently working on creating a list of our agency's fundamentals and will make these statements a major point of emphasis moving forward. The book describes fundamentals as "a specific methodology and set of tools for creating and institutionalizing an organization's culture."[33] For us, this is a natural next step to follow building our culture upon our mission and values. One fundamental we had already been using was the "make it better" fundamental (I had no idea it was a "fundamental" when we came up with it). An example of another one that is used in the book, which we will definitely add to our list is, "Blameless problem-solving." I love that one! Once you get the book and follow their eight-step, practical process, you will then have several fundamentals that should become a part of your mission-minded language. Read the book. It can be a game changer for your organization.

Tell Me a Story

Telling stories can help drive home your mission. I have found that effective leaders are often good storytellers in general. Be intentional in the stories you tell and where you tell them. For me, there are two groups of stories; stories that I read or hear from other sources, and the stories of our people. When I read, I am intentional in notating stories I can use with our team. Remember the stories I shared earlier about President Eisenhower? I read those in a book written about his life. When I read those stories, I highlighted them

---

[33] Friedman, *Culture by Design.*

because I knew they could illustrate the importance of leadership engagement. I used those stories with our leadership team, and I continually use those stories when I teach as well. The same goes with the Dream Team story on purpose. I had never heard that story until I read a book on building effective teams at work. I recently told that story when kicking off our latest leadership book group. This is one of many reasons why I believe leaders are readers (you'll see that in the next section).

Regarding stories about your people, use them every chance you get. The more you reward employees for accomplishing the mission, the more stories you have to add to your cache of purpose-driven examples provided by your own people! I always encourage our employees at all levels to share stories of people meeting the mission. The main reason I ask for this is to be sure we can recognize our employees fulfilling our purpose. However, it also expands my file of employee stories that I can use in a variety of ways to emphasize our *why*.

Recognizing Mission Accomplished

As I said before, you likely have awards or methods of recognition that recognize a job well done. This is important. Don't ever stop celebrating employees doing their job well. Also, you should consider adding one more award or recognition method that is specifically related to an employee demonstrating your organization's purpose and values. Some good examples of this have already been provided. Think about those purpose-driven hospital cleaners or the cathedral builder working for "the Almighty." When employees clearly demonstrate your team's mission being met, recognize their willingness to be so purpose driven.

We use a challenge coin to specifically recognize employees displaying our purpose. We call it a Chief's Coin, and I am the only one that can present it to our employees. It has our patch on one side, our badge on the other side, and the words "Quality of Life" printed on it. Employees are encouraged to send me nominations of employees that should be celebrated for meeting our mission. Remember the two officers taking the four-year-old to her mother? Chief's Coin. A group of firefighters who responded to a medical call of an elderly man living at an assisted living facility with no family and found his room was in need of a deep clean? You guessed it—they took the time to clean it. Chief's Coin. Two police officers who helped a stranded motorist and found out they worked for a food delivery company and took the food to the person who ordered it? Chief's Coin (imagine being the citizen that came to the door and found a police officer there to deliver their lasagna). Get creative... come up with a specific way of recognizing your people meeting the mission. Make a big deal of it.

Mission on Display

If I walked into your building, would I have any idea what the why of your organization is and what it values? If possible (I know this could be difficult in some work environments), let your walls do the talking. If you have any artifacts that relate to your purpose or values, put them on display as well. You can just start by printing or framing your mission statement and placing a few copies in strategic locations.

We value our people. When you come to our headquarters or our fire stations, you will see pictures of our people at work. We got intentional and had a couple of employees who were also skilled photographers take some impressive photos of our people in action. Now, when you walk down our hallways, you see numerous pictures of our most prized asset—our people! We also have our mission statement in a few locations, including on the main wall of our headquarters lobby where citizens and visitors can clearly see it as soon as they walk into our building.

Debriefs

If you don't currently use intentional gatherings to discuss your team's previous work, handling of an incident, completion of a project, etc., you are missing a good opportunity. This is a great way to ensure you are always looking for ways to "make it better." As a team, discuss what was done well, what needs to be improved on, and also determine if the mission was met. If not, how can you be sure it is the next time?

Welcome to Our Mission

You hope your current employees will demonstrate and share your purpose with your new people. Beyond that, be intentional in including your purpose in your onboarding process. Come up with some good onboarding swag that displays your mission. Our leaders do a great job of taking our new employees to lunch on their first day. They ensure that this time is used to drive home what matters to us, and why we do what we do. As you train your new employees, be sure and make your purpose a big part of that training.

PART FOUR

3P LEADERSHIP— PASSION

"**Passionate leaders will increase the likelihood that those they influence are passionate as well.**"

Chapter 11

A PENCHANT FOR PASSION

SOME OF THE greatest examples of compelling force leaders were so influential because they were passionate. Passionate about helping others, passionate about making the world a better place, passionate about their personal convictions. Martin Luther King Jr. was passionate about civil rights. Mahatma Gandhi was passionate about freeing his people from the British Empire. Mother Teresa was passionate about serving the poorest of the poor. Abraham Lincoln was passionate about freeing slaves. Nelson Mandela was passionate about fighting apartheid.

Passion and compelling force leadership go hand in hand. As a matter of fact, regarding 3P Leadership, we almost have a little bit of the chicken and the egg thing going. Can you add value to *p*eople by leading with *p*urpose effectively without *p*assion? Not really. Yet, adding value to *p*eople by leading with *p*urpose can also create *p*assion for you as a leader. Regardless, I truly believe all three aspects of transformational leadership connect (hence . . . the 3P Leadership approach). You can certainly debate how important passion is regarding quality leadership, but I will argue that if you want to sustain being the kind of leader we describe in this book, you have to have your heart in the right place. It's important to have a love for what you do.

Another passionate, and very successful leader, Steve Jobs, said the following in his commencement speech at a Stanford University graduation in 2005.

> Your work is going to fill a large part of your life, and the only way to be truly satisfied is to do what you believe is great work. And the only way to do great work is to love what you do. If you haven't found it yet, keep looking. Don't settle. As with all matters of the heart, you'll know when you find it.[34]

Steve stole my thunder. You need to believe that what you do is "great work" (purpose), and you need "to love what you do" (passion). Ultimately, passion will lead you to accomplish more than simply meeting the expectations of your role on the team. It will help push you to invest in what you do and invest in the people that help you do it. The second tenet of transformational leadership, inspirational motivation, will not come to fruition if you lack heart and passion. Can a leader be a somewhat effective manager without passion? Sure. Can a leader lack passion and add value to his or her people through building a healthy organization? Not likely.

We must also consider the impact a leader's passion can have on those on their team or in the organization. Science Direct describes emotional contagion as "a phenomenon of an automatic adoption of an emotional state of another person."[35] In other words, people's behavior is impacted by other people's emotional state. For example, imagine you have had a lousy day at work, and you are frustrated and tired. You get home and your wife tells you that you both have been invited to go to the neighbor's house for a cookout. You reluctantly go, and when you get there, you see several of your friends laughing and having a good time. You smell burgers cooking on the grill, and you all of a sudden start forgetting about your bad day as your mood

---

[34] Steve Jobs, "'You've Got to Find What You Love,' Jobs Says," Stanford News, August 24, 2022, https://news.stanford.edu/2005/06/12/youve-got-find-love-jobs-says/.

[35] "Emotional Contagion." Emotional Contagion - an overview | ScienceDirect Topics. Accessed March 16, 2023.
https://www.sciencedirect.com/topics/psychology/emotional-contagion.

brightens. Before you know it, you are smiling and laughing with the rest of the group. Although you are not aware of it, you experienced emotional contagion. It's important to be cognizant of the emotional impact our moods and behavior have on others, especially those we lead. Passionate leaders will increase the likelihood that those they influence are passionate as well.

Research has demonstrated a direct correlation between a leader's work passion and employee's work passion. As a leader, your attitude and passion about your work will likely be transferred to your followers via emotional contagion. One specific research project conducted on this topic found that a leader's passion influenced employee passion even more when there was congruence between leader and employee goals.[36] What this tells us is that when leaders are able to create a shared purpose between the leader and his or her team, and they display passion about that purpose, those team members are more likely to be passionate about the purpose as well.

Unfortunately, passion is not always present in our jobs. Many of you reading this right now are thinking to yourselves, "It's all I can do to get through the day . . . forget loving what I do!" Just today, my "passion" and "love for my job" took a gut punch first thing this morning. There have been several days during my time of writing this book where I almost felt hypocritical because I was not exactly overflowing with this passion I am preaching. However, I can honestly say that overall, I do love what I do, and I am passionate about it, and that helps sustain me during those times when I question if I am in the right place. If you truly love what you do, who you do it with, and why you do it, I can almost guarantee you there is light at the end of the tunnel of those dark times when every aspect of the job feels like a constant struggle. Passion keeps us fueled in our role as leaders and

---

[36] Li, Jingjing, Jian Zhang, and Zhiguo Yang. "Associations between a Leader's Work Passion and an Employee's Work Passion: A Moderated Mediation Model." Frontiers in psychology. U.S. National Library of Medicine, August 28, 2017. https://www.ncbi.nlm.nih.gov/pmc/articles/PMC5581499/.

helps our people maintain their passion though emotional contagion.

Like every area of leadership, there are some actions you need to be intentional in implementing to ensure your passion continues to provide the energy you need to lead others effectively. Before we tackle the areas of leading yourself in order to keep that passion lit, let's examine some passion extinguishers.

ARE YOU IN THE RIGHT PLACE?

We often talk about good leaders being willing to have courageous conversations with their people. Although most of us don't like these types of interactions, there is a tremendous benefit to having tough talks if the intent is to help people grow and improve, and if the person on the receiving end of such talk is open to taking that information and using it productively. Well, if you have no passion or love for your job, it may be time to have a courageous conversation with yourself.

We will soon discuss what can crush your love for what you do. However, the people and problems that can reduce our passion can be counteracted by specific methods of leading ourselves. But if you truly don't love (even like) what you do, you need to ask yourself if you are in the right place. If you feel like you are banging your head against the wall every day you come to work, is it time to consider finding a place with a different set of walls? Don't get me wrong, even if you hate your job, I know there is a lot to consider when it comes to trying to make a change—starting with being able to feed your family and pay the bills. Yet, if you find yourself in a leadership position, and you don't like what you do or where you do it, you are potentially hurting a lot of other people. It's one thing to have a sales job you don't enjoy. It's a completely different issue when you are leading a sales team and don't like what you do. You are probably going to make life miserable for your team, and you are likely hurting your company's bottom line as well.

Please understand . . . there is nothing wrong with making a change, even later in life. I recently had a meeting with an owner of a company who was in his early fifties. Up until recently, he had been in another profession for most of his adult life and had been pretty successful at it. However, he told me he had gotten to a point where he no longer liked what he did, and he wanted to do something with his skills he felt "mattered more." He made the change, and he is now purpose-driven and passionate. And I must say, he is good at what he does.

Barry Sanders was one of the best running backs the NFL has ever seen. He is one of two tailbacks to average at least five yards a carry throughout his career. He was only five feet, eight inches tall, weighing 203 pounds, and yet he finished his career with 15,269 yards rushing, which is fourth on the NFL all-time rushing list. In all ten of his seasons played, he was selected to the Pro Bowl. As the 1999 season approached, Sanders shocked the football world when he announced his retirement. He was only thirty-one years old, and he could have gone on to break several records, including the record for all-time rushing yards. Yet, as he stated in his retirement announcement, he had lost his passion for the game:

> Shortly after the end of last season, I felt that I probably would not return for the 1999-2000 season. I also felt that I should take as much time as possible to sort through my feelings and make sure that my feelings were backed with conviction. Today, I officially declare my departure from the NFL.
>
> The reason I am retiring is simple: My desire to exit the game is greater than my desire to remain in it. I have searched my heart through and through and feel comfortable with this decision.

Could he have continued playing and likely earned millions of more dollars and broken more records? Yes. Would he have been fulfilled in doing so? Based on his words, no. Sometimes, it's okay to walk away and do something different. Based on what I have read about him in various publications, Sanders has had a very quiet life after retirement, focusing a good bit of his time on some charities he is passionate about. Good for him.

AN IMPORTANT DISTINCTION TO CONSIDER

When you are in a leadership position, and you don't care for what you do, is it due to not liking the profession, or due to the frustrations connected to your leadership role in that profession? Remember, being a leader does not equate to being in a specific leadership role. We need leaders at all levels of the organization. What I am talking about here is specific to recognized leadership *positions* in the organization. Recently, in a neighboring fire department, an executive command staff member stepped down from his role. He loved being a firefighter, but he did not love being in an administrative leadership position. So, he went back to doing what he loved. That's a win for him, and I imagine it's a win for the organization as well. Sometimes, people just assume the next step is to promote to a leadership position, and when they get there, they realize it's not for them. Again, there is nothing wrong with this. What is wrong is when people continue to work in a role that involves leading others, and while doing so, are making themselves and their people miserable.

Let me throw in a third possibility. Maybe you love your profession, and maybe you love being a leader in your profession. It is possible that where you work is simply the wrong fit. It could be their mission does not align with yours. Or, maybe what they value doesn't match what you value. Or what you believe is important for leadership does not seem to correlate with the leaders you work with or those that lead you. If you desire to be a part of a healthy culture with 3P, compelling force leadership, and that does not exist in your current job you may very well lose your love for what you do. Really, it could come down to the old dating breakup line, "It's not you, it's me." It could be you—it could be you just don't fit well in a leadership role—or it may just be time for a change. But it also may not be you. It could be the place you work is not a good fit, but you are still drawn to the profession, and you are still drawn to leadership.

So, if you have lost your love for the job, step back and examine your situation. Don't make any rash decisions. Don't be in a hurry. Talk to people you trust and the people that know you the best. Is it possible leadership is not for you? Yes. Is there a chance you just need a change of profession? Yes. Or, could it be you just need a change of scenery and there is another organization out there that is a better fit for your passion and purpose in leadership? Absolutely. In the practical points section at the end of this chapter, I'll give you some questions to ask yourself that can help you pinpoint if you fall into one of these three categories.

Ultimately, if you are reading a book on leadership, that tells me there is a pretty good chance you desire to be an effective leader. If you have gotten this far and are a believer in being a compelling force leader that focuses on his or her people while being purpose-driven, I can only assume that leadership is for you. If your level of passion and excitement for your job is lacking right now, that's okay. We have all been there. It's a part of the leadership journey. Let's look at some of the factors that could be diminishing your passion in your current role and then discuss some practical ways to offset those factors and reignite your fire.

NEGATIVE PEOPLE

They are everywhere. They love to complain. They actually do look a gift horse in the mouth. One of the greatest drains of positivity is negativity. There are some people in life you can give a one-hundred-dollar bill to, and they will complain that you did not give it to them in twenties. I can come to work in a good mood and ready to take on the day, and within ten minutes, get deflated by negativity. Mark Twain once said, "Don't walk away from negative people, run!" That is great advice, except we often can't always run away from the people we work with every day.

If you find yourself in the unfortunate situation of being inundated with negativity from coworkers, it can certainly dampen your enthusiasm for the job.

This can especially be the case for leaders. You pour your heart and soul into trying to create value for your people and sometimes all you get back are questions or complaints about why they did not get more. What we have to realize is that the negative people are not necessarily (at least hopefully not) representative of the attitude of your overall team. They, like so many other areas in our society, often have the biggest mouths but represent the smallest group of people. Don't get me wrong, we need to be cognizant of where the negativity is originating. We don't want to lead with our heads in the sand. But we also don't need to allow the negativity to move us off the mission and lessen our enthusiasm as purpose-driven leaders.

NO THANKS

Leadership literally is a thankless job at times. It's human nature to want to be appreciated. Many of you have probably read or heard about *The Five Love Languages* by Dr. Gary Chapman. The basic premise is we each have our own love language that guides how loved or valued we feel by others. The five love languages include acts of service, receiving gifts, quality time, words of affirmation, and physical touch.[37] For me, my primary language is words of affirmation. So, what someone says, or does not say, will go a long way in how much I feel valued or appreciated. I have learned that this may not be the best love language to have as a leader (if I was writing this in a text or email, I would follow it with a LOL). There is some humor there, but honestly some truth as well.

There have been a few times when I fought hard to get our people what I thought was a big win and felt strongly it would

---

[37] "What Are the 5 Love Languages?," Discover Your Love Language - The 5 Love Languages®, https://5lovelanguages.com/learn.

move the needle. I ended up disappointed when they did not throw me the parade I thought I deserved. Actually, a parade was not even necessary, just a small token of appreciation would have been great. Nothing. But here's the problem with *my* disappointment in those situations. I was making it about *me*. If my motive for taking care of my people is to be recognized for it, my motive is in the wrong place. Don't get me wrong, a heartfelt thank you goes a long way, but that should not be why I do what I do as a leader. Our job is to show appreciation for our people, not seek it. We can't let a lack of gratitude from our team derail our passion for what we do. And, most of us have some people that do express their appreciation. When you get it, appreciate it. Just don't depend on it.

LACK OF PROGRESS

We have covered the value of being mission-minded in great detail. It is a vital part of compelling force leadership. However, when we fail to meet the mission, it can take the wind out of our sails. Often, leaders come into their role with visions of grandeur on how they can "make it better" for their team, division, or agency. Unfortunately, it often does not work out as we hoped. There are several reasons why this happens. Sometimes, it is as simple as we fail. We make mistakes. We don't always forecast well. Maybe we didn't effectively plan or budget appropriately. Sometimes we just don't get the job done. That's a part of leading—failing. Hopefully, we use those opportunities to grow and get better.

There are also times when the mission is not accomplished because of things out of our control. A leader can be a strategic genius and excellent planner and still fail to achieve goals that have been set. There may be budget issues, staffing shortages, and unexpected challenges (Covid-19) that slow down or completely derail progress. Most of the time, success is contingent upon a group of people working together and effectively fulfilling their roles to progress as an organization. Unfortunately, that can take a while to occur, and other people can greatly impede fulfillment of the organization's purpose. Again, out of your control.

Our purpose should drive everything we do. We need to set goals. We need to raise expectations. We need to have a vision of where we want to be and at least somewhat of an idea of how to get there. Conversely, we do NOT need to be naïve about how easy it will be to accomplish everything we set out to do. Set the bar high, but at the same time, don't let failure to reach the bar crush your leadership spirit. I can't guarantee many things about your leadership journey, but one thing I can promise is you will experience setbacks, and it will be painful at times.

If you happened to grow up in the eighties and listened to a lot of music (still the best music of all time), you knew who Casey Kasem was. He hosted *American Top 40* on radio stations across the country, and back then, teenagers made this weekly show a regular part of their listening routine. What song would be number one this week? What songs would break into the top forty, and what songs would drop out? Important stuff, I can assure you. Anyway, he always ended each show with a cheesy line that became his most popular catchphrase. He would sign off with, "Keep your feet on the ground and keep reaching for the stars." I mean . . . it does not get much sappier than that. I do think there is a nugget of wisdom for us in that phrase. Dream big, be mission-minded and keep working toward fulfilling the purpose of your organization. But do so while grounded in reality—and the reality is you will have setbacks and you will fail. If you accept this as a part of being a leader, your passion can actually sustain you through those times.

DEMANDS OF THE JOB

Work can be stressful, especially when part of your job is being responsible for the work other people are doing. Let's be real, leading is all about people, but leading people also creates a lot of demands on us. I have wondered what it would be like to have one of those jobs where you basically work by yourself and only have to be concerned about fulfilling specific tasks. Indeed.com listed the occupation of pet sitting as the number one job for working alone. I love the duties they list for the job; "A pet sitter supervises house pets while the pet owners are away by providing the animals with food and water. Pet sitters also provide care by walking and grooming the animals as needed."[38] Literally, you only have to be concerned with pleasing the pet owner and taking care of the pet. They listed the average pay as $48,072. This is a perfect example of a job that probably does not have a lot of demands on the person doing it. Take care of our dog, and we will pay you. Give me an old lazy, Labrador, and I'm in!

Now, take a midlevel manager. They have to lead and inspire their people to meet the mission, while at the same time meeting the demands placed on them by their bosses, and sometimes their bosses' bosses. And, if they are in some type of customer service business, they also have demands coming straight from the customers. Even CEOs, or chiefs like me, have demands coming from boards, elected officials, customers, citizens, and the people in our organizations. That's a lot of stress, which can equate to a loss of enthusiasm for the job. If a leader finds themselves in the unfortunate situation where unreasonable demands are being placed upon them, that can lead to a professional crisis and can certainly crush a leader's passion.

Having demands placed on us is a part of life at work. Part of the problem may be the way we handle those demands. For instance, we can be guilty of overscheduling and putting too much on our plates. Maybe we need an Organization 101 class to help us create some much-needed balance at work. Also, some people may be placing unrealistic demands on us, and they may not be aware what they are asking us is unreasonable. There may be a need to set expectations and engage in more effective communication with those we work with or for, which can help ensure

---

[38] Jamie Birt, "19 Best Jobs Where You Can Work Alone | Indeed.com - Indeed Career Guide," Indeed, June 22, 2022, https://www.indeed.com/career-advice/finding-a-job/jobs-where-you-work-alone.

reasonable expectations are established. Or, the people wearing you out may not care, and it may be time to look for another organization to utilize your time and talents.

PERSONAL PROBLEMS

Although it is ideal to separate work and home life, it is not always possible. Once again, we see a little bit of the chicken and the egg thing here. Stress in our personal life can create stress at work. Also, if we are stressed and burned out at work, this can create problems at home. I tell people I hire that this job is one of the noblest, most important jobs in the world . . . however, it is not more important than your family. With that said, even when people are struggling with personal issues, they still have to be able to work to support their families and pay the bills. We try to be generous when possible to allow employees to do what they need to do to take care of things in their personal life. In our profession, this can be tough because we also have to have people available to take care of our community twenty-four hours a day, seven days a week.

The role of taking care of employees can also create a dynamic in our leadership that can be especially taxing. We not only need to be looking out for our people and trying to make sure they are where they need to be mentally and emotionally, but we also have to make sure we are looking out for ourselves. We often focus on helping our teams and neglect our own wellness and our own families—which can be detrimental. I am constantly telling our people that when they are off, they need to disconnect from work. My leadership team however is quick to point out that I don't exactly practice what I preach in this area, and unfortunately, they are often right.

The whole next chapter focuses on ways to ensure there is a healthy balance between personal life and work life. This topic is something you could write an entire book on (like many other topics we cover in this book). I think it's safe to say there is great danger in derailing our careers if we don't focus on prioritizing what's important in our lives and keeping the main thing the main thing. Stress in our personal lives can certainly diminish our love for our jobs, but often a major source of that stress comes from not effectively focusing on what's most important in life. We have all met those people that find their identity in their jobs. That's not healthy, and usually, that does not end well, especially for families. We are much more apt to keep our passion for people and purpose at work when we are resolute in keeping our priorities in life in the correct order.

PRACTICAL POINTS

Before I add some practical questions to ask yourself and suggestions to counteract those areas that can diminish your passion, let me encourage each of you to go to workinggenius.com and do the working genius assessment for yourself. I mentioned this tool earlier in the book, and I believe it's a great assessment for everyone to take so you can know how your people are wired, and where they will be most passionate and productive at work. However, as you have that courageous conversation with yourself regarding if you are in the right place, this tool can help you see if you are in a position or organization where you are more or less apt to be passionate and productive. Do the assessment and read the book, or at least read the explanations of each genius on the website and see where you are most likely to love what you do.

Now, let's look at some questions to ask yourself and some ways to deal with those things at work that can diminish your passion for people and purpose:

Am I in the right job/profession? Some questions to consider:

- Do I dread coming to work every day?
- Do I feel like what I do is important?
- If I started over tomorrow, would I choose this profession?

- Would I recommend my job to a close friend?
- Have I lost the joy I once had at work?
- Has my job decreased my joy outside of work?
- Do I feel disengaged at work?
- Do I feel stuck at work?

Please note: If you are not in the right job, don't just assume you need to get totally out of the profession. Look at the questions below related to being a leader and your current organization. The profession may still be right for you, but maybe your frustration is more connected to a leadership role or where you go to work every day. I don't want anyone jumping the gun and going in tomorrow and quitting (especially with no game plan). We all have bad days and weeks, but if you have been struggling for a while, then step back and take a holistic view of your work circumstances. Hopefully, there are some actions you can take to reignite your passion as a compelling force leader. But if your issues are bigger and broader than that, it would behoove you to really step back and closely examine your current profession and your options for the future.

Is a leadership position for me? Maybe you are like the firefighter I previously mentioned . . . you love the job, just not _leading_ in the job. Some questions to ask:

- What was my motive for taking a leadership role in the first place? Was it for the perks, because it was the natural "next step," or to improve my organization?
- Am I interested in how the organization operates?
- Am I comfortable, or interested in, taking on administrative tasks?
- Do I enjoy helping other people grow and develop?
- Do I have a clear leadership philosophy?
- Do I read and study leadership?
- Am I a strategic thinker?

If you are in the right profession, and you feel like a leadership role is for you, you need to ask some questions about your organization:

- Do my organization's values align with mine?
- Do I feel like I have to compromise my principles in order to be successful at work?
- Are my leaders investing in my growth and development?
- Am I unclear on the purpose or *why* of the organization I work for?
- Do I feel undervalued?
- Would I recommend my agency to my friends looking for a job?
- Do I feel like organizational leadership does not care about my work-life balance?

Hopefully, you still feel like you want to be in a leadership role, in your profession, and where you currently work. If that's you, here are some practical ways to deal with the passion killers that almost all leaders wrestle with from time to time.

Negative People

A key to dealing with the effects of negative people is to limit how many negative people you have at work, especially in crucial positions. Once again, it is extremely important that we hire and promote the right people. As far as hiring people that are a good fit, do your best to talk to previous managers and coworkers that have worked with the candidates you are considering. Have potential candidates spend some time with some of your compelling force personnel that can provide you with some honest feedback. People trying to get a job will always put their best foot forward during interviews with their potential bosses. However, if you can get them with their potential peers and help them drop their guard, there is a better chance of them showing their true colors, including their attitudes and propensity to be a negative employee.

We now require police candidates who are going through our hiring process to ride a few hours with one of our officers on duty. We, of course, are strategic in which officers we choose to engage with police officer candidates. I recently called one of these officers who had a candidate ride with him to get his feedback because our hiring team had some concerns about this candidate. I asked for his honest assessment, and he shared with me his concerns that aligned with the concerns others had described. So, in spite of doing very well in the interview process, we did not hire him. Try to be intentional in creating opportunities for people you are considering for hire to engage with some of your best people for a period of time. The feedback you get from your people can be very helpful in ensuring you are hiring men and women that are a right fit for your culture, while also helping you avoid hiring negative, energy drainers.

It is vitally important that you promote people that fit your purpose and enhance people's passion, not diminish it. The last thing you want is to promote whiners and complainers that are going to negatively impact the people they influence. These types of people serving in leadership roles are culture killers. As previously stated, that is why it is so important to get feedback from other people they have worked with, and for, if possible. Again, be strategic in your promotional process to ensure you get a well-rounded perspective on candidates you are considering for promotion. You do not want to promote people with a negative bent. Even if they excel in other areas, they will do more damage than good if they are placed in crucial leadership roles.

As far as dealing with current employees or leaders that are negative, try to consider their motivation for being so negative. Talk to them and attempt to determine what is at the core of their negativity. Is it possible they are just negative because that's who they are? Of course. Is it also possible they are negative because of their work environment? Yes. You might find their negativity is somewhat justified because of factors you may or may not have been aware existed. Just showing a sincere interest in what's bothering them and a willingness to listen to them, can sometimes result in immediate improvement.

Additionally, this may be a chance for you or your team to learn about some areas where improvement or change is needed. I try to consider the source of direct criticism toward me. Even when I feel the source is way off base or completely irrational, I always try (yes, *try* . . . not saying I actually always do it) to look for things I can improve on moving forward. The same can go for dealing with negative people at work. Even if their negativity is a "them" problem, sometimes, we can glean certain ways we might improve ourselves or our organization.

For those people that are going to be negative regardless of their circumstances or environment, do all you can to limit their exposure to yourself and others, assuming you don't have a valid reason to just let them go. It's not always an option, but if you can put them on an island, in a role that has limited contact with others, do it. Also, they need to understand that their attitude is not acceptable. When appropriate, start documenting incidents where their negativity had a—well—negative impact on other employees or your team in general. If they are not willing to change their behavior, once you have clearly expressed your expectations, you need to begin to build a case for an eventual separation of employment. Oftentimes, they will leave on their own when they realize their behavior will no longer be tolerated. If they don't choose to leave, you may eventually have to make that choice for them.

No Thanks

Compelling force, transformational leaders don't do what they do for praise. That being said, words of gratitude can fuel our passion for adding value to others. When those words are absent, especially during trying times, it's easy to lose enthusiasm. The old "it's lonely at the top" adage is often true, especially when it comes to feeling appreciated. The only practical advice I can give here is to find your appreciation in other sources. From time to time, give yourself a chance to reflect on what has been achieved. Make sure you utilize the thirty-thousand-foot view to see the good of what has been accomplished, not just the areas where goals have not been met.

Avoiding the negative people, and being intentional in surrounding yourself with positive, affirming people when possible will also keep your love for leading strong. There is a group of leaders in our profession, all from other agencies, who I meet with once a month. We all share the same faith, values, and view of leadership. We usually go through a leadership book together. The true value of getting together is really found in the fact that we can all relate to and appreciate the struggles of leadership. We also appreciate each other. I leave those early morning gatherings each month refueled and regenerated. As you focus on engaging with your people, also take time to engage with people who fill your tank.

Lack of Progress

Most leaders are visionary and goal-oriented. When they fail to meet those goals in a timely manner, it can certainly create frustration and stifle their passion for leading. I am a huge big-picture guy, and when things are not happening the way I envision them needing to happen, it's tough sometimes. Throw in some impatience, and it can definitely lead to some disheartening periods in the leadership journey.

Honestly, one of the best remedies for this is experience. The longer you work in leadership, the more you understand how to focus on reasonable expectations. If you constantly look at the big picture, especially when you are trying to change the culture of a team or organization, you will lose sight of the wins. If we focus more on the small wins, that will help us see the organization is moving forward. Setting grand goals is good, but don't hesitate to set some smaller goals as well. Sometimes, we truly do miss the trees when all we focus on is the forest. When you have those small wins, notate them and celebrate them. Keep a journal of your achievements, no matter how small they may seem. If you are having an especially deflating day, refer to your recent wins. At times, at the end of staff meetings, I will ask our leadership team to tell me something good. They will share stories of things that are going well. Those are wins. We focus a lot on what needs to be done, which is a must for leadership. Just be sure and give yourself a few moments to focus on the achievements, big or small, as well.

Demands of the Job

Some demands you simply cannot control. Deadlines set by others that you must follow, orders that must be filled in a timely manner, and personnel voids that must be filled in order to operate effectively and efficiently. Part of leading is dealing with the demands of the job. The problem comes when we are constantly feeling like we are just barely keeping our heads above water. No matter how good you may be at treading water, eventually, you are going to get worn down and tired, and if you are not careful, start swallowing too much water.

Going back to Covey's concept of what we can control and what we cannot . . . start examining what you *can* control related to meeting the demands you can't. In other words, what can you do better to manage the expectations that are associated with your job? I shared earlier how ridiculously busy I was when I first started in my current role. What I eventually realized was a lot of that was my fault. I have always prided myself on being fairly organized, including in how I manage my time. I discovered that my new role placed more demands on me than any other role I had ever filled. So, maybe I was not as good as I thought when it came to being an effective manager of time. I had to be much more intentional in balancing my calendar. I can tell you that my enthusiasm for my job is much higher when I am not burning the candle at both ends at work. If you are struggling in this area, maybe look at taking a time management course, or working with someone that demonstrates strong time management skills.

There are also times when you can control what tasks you accept. One of the challenges for new leaders is they often still want to do the job they now are supposed to be leading other people to do. Leaders that have always been doers often struggle with letting go of some of their former tasks and responsibilities. In their mind, it's easier to do it themselves. That is a great indicator of a hard worker, but also often an indicator of an ineffective leader. Plus, if you are always trying to do everything yourself, you are going to burn out eventually, and you are not creating opportunities for your people to develop and grow. Burned-out leaders are not passionate leaders. You have to learn to spread the work and delegate when appropriate. Again, experience helps with this. If there is more work than you can handle, what tasks can you delegate for others to accomplish? I can tell you when I finally got to a point where I was utilizing my team to handle certain tasks, this led me to being a much more engaged and energized leader.

Finally, just say no. You can't do it all. Don't say yes to every opportunity that comes your way. We don't always have a choice regarding what our job entails. But there are times when we do have options. Don't over-extend yourself. If you are doing too much and getting burned out, look at your responsibilities and see what you can omit. If you are offered an opportunity to engage in a new endeavor, ask yourself some questions. Does this fit *my* purpose as a leader? Will it add value to my team or the people I work for or serve? Will this take more time away from my family and other people that are important to me? Will saying yes create more passion, or add more stress to my life? From time to time, I get asked to serve on panels or boards. I used to say yes to almost everything. I have learned (again ... experience) to be more particular about when to say yes.

Personal Problems

See the next chapter ...

Chapter 12

KEEPING THE SAW SHARP

I LIVE IN a large neighborhood with a very *active* HOA. They don't miss much when it comes to residents adhering to the neighborhood covenants. Apparently, they are well versed in the area of arborist work, as they identified a tree in my yard that needed to be removed because it was dying. I discovered this via one of their official "you need to take care of this or else" letters. Now, I am no expert when it comes to trees, or anything else that grows out of the ground for that matter, but when I looked at the tree they demanded be removed, it looked perfectly fine to me. The tree was only about six inches in diameter and approximately twelve feet tall. I mean, who are these people to tell me I should cut down a perfectly nice-looking tree? I guess someone on the board knew what they were talking about because a few weeks later, it became obvious the tree was indeed dying. Even then, I pulled the typical "I'll get to it later"-man approach to household jobs until it really got bad, and we were having several family members coming over for Mother's Day.

So, the Saturday before Mother's Day, I decided this was the day to remove the tree that had garnered the attention of the HOA timber police. Unfortunately, I did not have a chainsaw at that time. Why would I? I live in a five-hundred-home subdivision in the suburbs, not a forest. For you guys that are thinking I should have my man card removed, don't judge me. Anyway, I have a friend who owns a landscaping company, so I called him and asked if I could borrow one of his chainsaws (I may not have one, but I do know how to operate one). He obliged and dropped one off that morning. So I cranked it up and got to work. I was assuming it would take less than a minute to cut down the tree since it was not very big. Unfortunately, after about five minutes of furious work and manhandling the chainsaw, there were no substantial results. Eventually, I got down on one knee and started trying to put some muscle behind the chainsaw, but once again, with very little progress to show for it. At this point, I thought my neighbors were watching me and thinking to themselves, *why can't this moron cut down such a small tree?* After about ten minutes of sweating and straining, trying different angles, and mumbling several words under my breath I am not going to print here, I threw down the chainsaw and went and got my axe. That's right . . . real men have axes.

I eventually got the tree down with the axe and dragged it to the back of my property for an eventual trip to the landfill. When my friend came back later, I told him about my horrible experience with his chainsaw and explained how it was completely useless. He examined it closely and started laughing. I, of course, did not see any humor in the situation and asked him what was so funny. He responded that he accidentally gave me one of his chainsaws that was out of service because the blade was completely dull. I was frustrated and relieved at the same time. It was not my fault . . . it was faulty equipment! I wanted to go and tell all my neighbors that may have seen me, but then I realized that would just be weird. By the way, I now own a chainsaw.

The moral of the story is this: a dull blade is useless. You can keep trying over and over again, but it still won't cut. You can try different approaches to using it or try to muscle up to make it work. But if it's not sharp, it's not going to do the job. The same goes for leaders. If you are dull, your effectiveness in leading others will be sluggish. If we are not careful, we can get worn down and dull and not only lose our zeal for the job but also become inadequate in adding value to our people. It's incumbent upon us to keep ourselves sharp, primarily because that is what our people deserve. When we accepted the responsibility of leadership, we committed to consistently giving our absolute best to those we have the privilege of serving. I listed some of the passion killers in the previous chapter. If we let those people and circumstances get the best of us, we will lose our passion for leading others. Like so many other areas of leadership, we need to be proactive in making sure we stay sharp, which will help ensure we are adding value to people by leading with purpose and passion. Compelling force leaders that excel in leading others are also able to lead themselves.

In this chapter, I want to get down to the basics of leading ourselves. Honestly, leading ourselves in these four areas will not only help us stay sharp at work but in life in general. Full transparency, there was a time when I thought this topic was a good add-on to the other important tenets of leadership, but not overly important. I could not have been more wrong. I have learned that being intentional in leading myself will help ensure I prevent my blade from getting dull, even when dealing with the passion killers we previously discussed. In the next chapter, I will tackle another area in which we can lead ourselves. Let's first look at the four areas of self-leadership that need our initial focus.

PHYSICAL SHARPNESS

Heart disease runs rampant on my dad's side of the family. He has had open heart surgery and at least two heart attacks. Most of his many siblings have dealt with heart issues as well. Therefore, knowing heart disease is often hereditary, taking care of my heart is consistently at the top of mind for me, as well as my wife. I am extremely thankful for my wife for more reasons than I can list, but I am especially appreciative of her desire to keep me alive and healthy. I know her motives are sincere and pure when it comes to keeping me healthy because she is extremely loving and caring, and I have an ample life insurance policy that she would benefit from if I met my ultimate demise. With all that said, I have a strong understanding of the importance of exercising and taking care of myself physically, which is especially important when it comes to taking care of my heart.

Beyond the obvious health benefits that come with exercising, there is another huge benefit to engaging in physical exercise . . . it's a great stress reliever. Leadership and stress go hand in hand, which can contribute to creating a dull blade. We all need an outlet to help alleviate the negative impact stress has on us physically. Exercise is that outlet.

According to the Mayo Clinic, exercise pumps up our endorphins, which helps us feel good, while at the same time lowering cortisol, which is a known stress hormone. I am sure you have heard of a runner's high. That "high" comes from your production of endorphins. It also reduces the negative effects and improves your mood overall.[39] The American Psychological Association found that 62 percent of adults who exercise find it to be extremely effective in reducing stress.[40]

Another benefit to exercising that can help with stress is how it can impact our decision-making. According to a recent study, eighty minutes a week of exercise strongly improved decision-making.[41] If I am more effective at making decisions at work, and in life in general for that matter, would that reduce stress? You bet it would. Decision-making is one of the more stressful parts of leadership at times, and making better decisions will always be

---

[39] Mayo Clinic Staff, "Exercise and Stress: Get Moving to Manage Stress," Mayo Clinic (Mayo Foundation for Medical Education and Research, August 3, 2022), https://www.mayoclinic.org/healthy-lifestyle/stress-management/in-depth/exercise-and-stress/art-20044469.

[40] "Exercise: A Healthy Stress Reliever," American Psychological Association (American Psychological Association, 2014), https://www.apa.org/news/press/releases/stress/2013/exercise.

[41] Dolan, Eric W. "Physical Activity Can Improve Self-Controlled Decision Making, Study Finds." PsyPost, 1 Aug. 2017, https://www.psypost.org/2017/08/physical-activity-can-improve-self-controlled-decision-making-study-finds-49387.

beneficial. This is another indicator of what many of us already know is true. Exercise helps clear our minds. My routine is to exercise first thing in the morning. During the week, that means getting up really early. I can tell you, it's extremely hard most days to get going in the gym or starting a run. But once I put those AirPods in my ears and start exercising, my mind goes into neutral, and I check out mentally. For me, it's a great way to start my day because I feel a sense of accomplishment, and my mind is cleared as my day gets going. No matter what time of day works best for you, just know taking care of yourself physically through exercise will equate to an effective method of relieving stress. Less stress means a sharper saw.

SPIRITUAL SHARPNESS

When I teach about leaders leading themselves, I always provide a caveat for this section. I call this spiritual sharpness. You may see it the same way I do, or you may call it something else. Regardless, this is the area of leading ourselves that helps us keep things in proper perspective. As a man of faith, I see life through a specific lens. Ideally, my priorities are my faith, followed by my family, and then other areas like church, work, other relationships, etc. Although I don't always succeed in keeping my priorities in order, this area does help me keep the main thing the main thing. I love my job. I am extremely blessed to be able to do what I do. If I lost my job tomorrow, it would be very difficult. However, I would be fine in the long run because I don't connect my identity to my profession.

We all need something in our lives to keep things in proper perspective. For me, that's my faith. It's amazing how many people get caught up in the matters of life that often just aren't that important in the big scheme of things. This is clearly an issue in our society, and it can also be an issue at work. We can get really worked up about "problems" over which we have no control.

Let me bring Covey up one more time. We need to focus on what we can control and try not to concern ourselves about what we can't. Also, we all have a lot we can complain about at work. Honestly, many of us find ourselves in favorable conditions as work, and yet, we still manage to focus on what we don't have. Now, I am sure some of you reading this have legitimate, difficult work problems. But if we have a proper perspective on the big picture, we will often see that our situations are not as bad as they may seem, especially when we keep our priorities in order.

Recently, I attended the funerals of two Sheriff's deputies from the same department that were shot and killed serving a warrant. All of a sudden, my problems did not seem so bad as I watched wives, children, parents, and the brothers and sisters that wore the same patch as those heroes that lost their lives suffer in anguish over such a devastating loss. Those two men served in one of the noblest professions on the face of the planet, and they died serving their community. However, their roles as husbands, fathers, sons, and friends were much more important than their role as deputy sheriffs. It's all about perspective.

Life is too short to be worked up over work. So many people are dominated by their jobs. Trust me, it can happen easily. I have been very upfront about how stressful leadership can be at times. It is also a privilege to lead, and we should always try to keep the idealism of making a difference in the lives of others as a focal point in our approach to doing our jobs. I feel confident I am doing what God has called me to do, and that helps me keep things in a proper perspective. For you, determine what you need in your life to keep the main thing the main thing. If work is constantly overwhelming you, what changes do you need to establish in order to correct the unnecessary stresses that are dulling your blade? Our jobs are very important . . . but not worth negatively dominating our lives. Leaders with a healthy and balanced perspective are far more likely to be effective compelling force leaders. Maintaining the appropriate view of work and life will help you preserve the passion you need to lead people with purpose.

MENTAL SHARPNESS

As previously mentioned, I am a reformed hater of reading. In elementary, middle, and high school, I loathed reading. Even during my undergrad work in college, I despised it. I was the guy that would buy the cliff notes or watch the movie instead of actually reading a book. It wasn't until I found the value of reading leadership books that I found a love for reading. Now, I love reading many different styles of books, both nonfiction and fiction. As I stated at the beginning, I truly believe leaders are readers. If you are serious about growing as a compelling force leader, it will greatly benefit you to read what other successful compelling force leaders have to say about leadership.

There is now another reason I firmly believe it is important to consistently read. It sharpens our minds. Reading is an effective method of exercising our minds. Just like running or lifting weights improves our physical fitness, reading helps our mental fitness. As a guy who is in his early fifties (which is still very young by the way), my memory is not what it used to be, and to be honest, even in my prime, it was never that great. It's funny how I struggle to remember what I had for lunch yesterday, but I can remember that Jenny's number is 8-6-7-5-3-0-9 (that's for the readers that were raised on the radio in the eighties . . . I bet you will now have that song playing in your mind over and over again). Reading sharpens our minds and can help improve our memory and reduce cognitive decline, which can ensure we are effective at work and in life. A study published in 2020 showed that people who read once or more a week had less risk for cognitive decline. When we read, it increases the brain's electrical activity and helps push the brain to constantly make new connections, which in turn improves memory.[42]

If the thought of reading still makes you queasy, I have another suggestion for you. Technology is a beautiful thing. If you

---

[42] Lorea Lastiri, "Does Reading Improve Memory?," Iris Reading, February 3, 2022, https://irisreading.com/does-reading-improve-memory/.

hate reading, you can actually have people read to you! That's right, there's an app for that. While you are commuting to work, you can have people read books to you. Almost all mainstream books are available in some type of audio format. As far as I am concerned, listening to podcasts has similar benefits to listening to books. There are a lot of good podcasts on leadership available as well as several other interesting and entertaining topics.

RELATIONAL SHARPNESS

Harvard conducted a study that covers a period of seventy-nine years with the goal of determining what truly makes people happy. I think it is safe to assume this is a study we can take to the bank! In a 2015 TED Talk, Robert Waldinger, a professor at Harvard Medical School, shared the results of this study which tracked the lives of 724 men. What did the study ultimately find? After gathering tens of thousands of pages of research, the outcome was clear and simple. Waldinger stated, "Good relationships keep us happier and healthier."[43] An almost eight-decade-long Harvard study established that being connected with others is what makes people happy. Not money, not power, not prestige, not notoriety, not cool stuff, but people.

As a leader in the profession of public safety, I can assure you, this may sound and seem a little too touchy-feely. People that put their lives on the line, carry guns, and put out fires are not apt to discuss the importance of having healthy relationships. But I promise you, it does matter. The more we are connected with people, the better leaders we are, and the more we will optimize our life in general. Unfortunately, stress at work creates stress on relationships. Throw in crazy schedules, financial stress, and the safety concerns that come with protecting and serving the public, and it can be especially hazardous for family

---

[43] Zameena Mejia, "Harvard's Longest Study of Adult Life Reveals How You Can Be Happier and More Successful," CNBC (CNBC, March 20, 2018), https://www.cnbc.com/2018/03/20/this-harvard-study-reveals-how-you-can-be-happier-and-more-successful.html.

life. Relationships are already hard work, and work can make them even harder.

I'll revert back to what I said before, as important as your job may be, it is not more important than your family. You define what you consider family . . . spouse, children, siblings, parents, other family, friends etc. The people that should be a priority in your life should not be displaced by work. Total transparency here . . . I am not always very good at this. My family—my wife especially—has put up with a lot over the years. Although I strive to make sure my family comes first, I have often failed at making that actually come to fruition. My wife is a saint. She has and continues to put up with a lot when it comes to me not creating a healthy balance between home and work. I tell you this because I know, and I want you to know, that this is always something we have to work on improving. If we take our eye off the ball even a little, we can quickly make those important to us not feel very important.

And, if the only people you hang out with are the people you work with, that's not healthy. We all need to be connected with people not connected to our jobs. Investing our time into the people important to us will make us sharper. The goal is to connect with our families in a healthy manner because it's the right thing to do, not to make us better at work (check the motive). Family/important relationships should be first, and when we successfully prioritize those pertinent relationships in a consistent fashion, one of the positive results will be us moving closer to becoming effective compelling force leaders. You probably already know what you need to work on as it relates to this topic. You know what relationships are not getting the attention they deserve. You know what people in your life deserve more of your time and investment than what you are currently giving them. Let this be a reminder of the importance of connecting with the important people in your life. It's the right thing to do, and it's another area of leading yourself that will result in keeping you sharp.

PRACTICAL POINTS

Everyone is different. What may work for me in more effectively leading myself may not work for you. The overall goal is to create a game plan for growth and improvement in all of these areas. How can you "make it better" by ensuring your leadership saw stays sharp? I'll give a few suggestions and share a few things that have worked for me. A major component of finding success in leading yourself comes down to developing good habits. I highly recommend the book *Atomic Habits* by James Clear. It is a very practical book on habit formation. It's one of those books I know I should read from time to time to make sure I am staying on track regarding developing and maintaining healthy habits.

Physical Sharpness

Let's start with this question . . . are you doing any type of physical activity on a consistent basis? If the answer is no, then I would recommend setting a simple goal of thirty minutes of exercise, three days a week. If you are currently doing nothing, just start doing something three days a week. It can be as simple as taking a thirty-minute walk. Put on some headphones, turn on some good music or an entertaining podcast or book, and take a walk. From there, always work toward doing more. Next, try forty minutes. Maybe integrate some weights or bodyweight exercises as well. Move to four days a week. Keep increasing. Keep improving. There are a lot of free exercise plans online for people just getting started, or restarted, in the area of physical exercise. If you are already doing some exercise, set some goals and do a little more, or make it a little harder on yourself. The goal is to always increase and improve.

I would also recommend figuring out the best time of day to exercise. I am a morning exercise guy. This routine requires me getting my uniform or attire for the next day ready the night before, so I don't have to add that to my morning task list. Most weekday mornings, my routine is pretty consistent. I get up early, do some brief reading and have a devotion time, walk my dog, make some coffee, and head to work. Once I get to work, I either work out in our gym or go for a run. Some days I have to get up really early because of early morning meetings, and there are some days I just don't get it done. One thing I have learned about myself is that exercising in the evenings just does not work well for me. I would recommend you create a routine, at whatever time of day works for you, and make exercising a part of that routine. Most of us are not just going to work out, walk, or run on a whim. Creating habit-based routines will lead to us being more apt to staying committed to an exercise strategy.

Spiritual Sharpness

This is personal, and something you need to determine on your own. I would just recommend looking at your typical day to see what you need to change to ensure you elevate what's most important to the top of your priority list. As I said above, I try to start each day with a devotion to get my mind right and create the appropriate perspective for the day. I can't say I am always successful at it, but again, it's a part of my normal routine. Make sure you are strategic in creating time away from work and do the best you can to disconnect and spend some time engaging in activities that will keep your saw sharp.

Mental Sharpness

Similar to physical exercise, if you are not reading at all, just start trying to read three days a week, ten minutes at a time (I am really setting the bar low). Find a leadership book or utilize an app to have someone read to you. I actually try to have three books going at one time. I usually am reading a leadership book, a spiritual book, and something fictional or totally new. I do not hit all of these books each day, and there are several days when I end up not reading at all. Try to create a strategy for reading and stick to it. Set some goals and see what happens. Reading some is better than not reading at all.

Try to read some articles or books on something you know nothing about. It's great to read with the intention of learning new things in life. I have always had an interest in science, space, and technology. There are a couple of online sites I will go to from time to time to gain some new knowledge in these areas. This a great way to exercise and expand your mind.

Relational Sharpness

Again, this is very specific to your situation, and you likely have an idea of what you need to do to improve your relationships. My only suggestion . . . give more and do more. Give more time to the people important to you. Do more with and for your family and loved ones. As I said before, I am a task guy. I will think of something I can or need to do for someone I care about and ask Siri to set a reminder for me to make sure I follow through with it. If my wife makes a statement in passing that indicates something is meaningful or important to her, I will often create a reminder for the future). As leaders, we are often successful at being intentional at work. It's even more pertinent that we are intentional with the people who should matter the most to us.

Chapter 13

KEEP ON GROWING

IF YOU GREW up in the South as I did, there's a pretty good chance you know about kudzu. For those that don't know, it is almost impossible to kill. In the 1930s and '40s, farmers in the South were paid to plant kudzu to help slow down soil erosion. Eventually, over one million acres were planted. The problem is it became recognized as a "pest weed" in the 1950s. It's still alive and growing today. This vine, known by many as "the vine that ate the South" will kill native plants and even trees. Left unattended, kudzu will consistently continue to spread. Basically, it never stops growing. It can grow as much as a foot a day![44]

No matter where you are in your leadership journey, one of your goals should always be to continue to grow and develop as a leader. Don't ever stop growing. Even if you find yourself at the pinnacle level of John Maxwell's five levels of leadership, you have to continue to be intentional in looking for effective ways to "make it better" as a leader. This falls right in line with Sinek's assessment of quality leaders having the characteristics of humility and teachability. When you are humble, and you remain teachable, you will always have the potential to grow, develop, and learn new and more effective ways to lead. Show

---

[44] "Kudzu," Kudzu (Pueraria Montana var. lobata), https://www.invasive.org/alien/pubs/midatlantic/pumol.htm.

me leaders that thinks they have arrived and no longer need to worry about growing, and I will show you leaders that are quickly becoming obsolete and ineffective.

While doing some research for this book, I came across an organization called Growing Leaders: Ready for Life and their website, growingleaders.com. I don't know much about the organization, but I read an article on their site about the correlation between passion and learning. I completely agree with the statement in the article that said, "Passions emerge from the interests and issues that you are motivated to spend time learning more about."[45] That is so true. If you are passionate about leadership, you will grow that passion when you learn more about leadership.

When I started working in leadership roles, I developed an interest in the transformational leadership approach to leading, as I felt it was especially needed in our current work culture. However, I became even more passionate and excited about this topic when I spent numerous hours researching the subject when writing my dissertation. When I study and research leadership, it actually fuels my passion for leading others. When you are learning about something you love, it will enhance your passion, which in turn helps you grow.

I truly believe one of the ways we keep our saw sharp is by never being satisfied with the status quo. Compelling force leaders are always looking for ways—here it is again—to make it better. A very dangerous place for a leader to find him or herself is in the comfort zone. When we get comfortable and complacent, even when things are going well, our influence will begin to wane, and we are in danger of losing our edge. Being content where you are and having no desire to explore bigger and better ways of doing things will completely stifle leading yourself through growth and development.

The fire profession is extremely steeped in tradition. For the

---

[45] Chris Harris, "Passion and Leadership," Growing Leaders, April 4, 2019, https://growingleaders.com/passion-and-leadership/.

most part, it is one of the aspects of firefighting that makes it such a wonderful profession. There is a lot of pride associated with being a firefighter, and that is something leaders should be protective of . . . to a certain degree. There is a fine line between doing what we do because of tradition, and doing what we do "because we have always done it that way." In the fire profession, and in any other profession, operating a certain way only because that is the way it has always been done is far from a growth and development mindset. Tradition can be incorporated in our organizations, but if we are not careful, it can prevent our teams, units, and agencies from being innovative and open to mechanisms that will ultimately provide improvement and growth. It is especially important that leaders avoid the "we have always done it this way" mindset. As a matter of fact, we often have to fight against the natural pull towards the status quo for the betterment of our teams.

There is a well-known experiment that supposedly took place at the University of Wisconsin-Madison in 1966 involving five monkeys. These five monkeys were put into a large cage with a ladder in the middle of it. The ladder led up to some hanging bananas. As you can imagine, it did not take long for one of the monkeys to climb the ladder to retrieve the bananas. As that first monkey began his climb, the experimenter sprayed that monkey, and the other four monkeys, with cold water. The climber immediately came back down with no bananas, and there was a cage full of wet and cold monkeys. Eventually, a second monkey decided to take a shot at the bananas with the same results, five wet and cold monkeys with no bananas. Now, here is where it starts to get interesting. A third started climbing the ladder and the other four monkeys, who were obviously tired of getting sprayed with cold water, grabbed the other monkey, pulled him back down, and gave him a butt whipping.

The next phase of the experiment involved replacing one of the original five monkeys with a new monkey. As you would expect, he wanted to get the bananas, and when he started climbing, the same butt-whipping occurred at the hands of the other four monkeys. Then, a second new monkey was put into the cage with another original being removed. You guessed it, ladder climb lead to a pummeling. This continued until none of the original monkeys were left and there were five new monkeys who had never been sprayed with cold water and had no interest in going for the bananas. If you could ask the monkeys why they did not go for the bananas, their response (maybe in sign language) would be, "We really don't know why we don't go after the bananas, but that is the way we have always done it."[46] The lesson here for all of us is to constantly examine why we do what we do, with the goal of growing and getting better in mind. If you are choosing to not go for the bananas, but you really don't know why you are making that choice, you are choosing the status quo over leading yourself and your agency in maintaining a growth mindset.

In trying to engage in a mentality that is always growth-centric, you can follow the steps we discussed earlier on how you can ensure you are developing your people. Three of those steps . . . education, evaluation, and emulation all can be utilized as tools for leading yourself through growth and development. Let's look at how each of these development approaches can be catered to your growth and development as you try to keep yourself sharp.

EDUCATION

I mentioned earlier the importance of investing in our people through training. Well, the same development discipline should apply to you. You need to ensure you are also investing in your own development through leadership education. We often push others to train, but don't push ourselves to do the same. Busyness

---

[46] Russ Gambrel, "5 Monkeys in a Cage (and One Important Business Lesson)," Fahrenheit Advisors, August 27, 2019,
https://fahrenheitadvisors.com/advisory-news/5-monkeys-in-a-cage-and-one-important-business-lesson-by-russ-gambrel/.

and boredom can be two roadblocks to educating ourselves as leaders. It is tough to set aside time for training because we are busy. This goes back to having a good balance at work so you can create time for you to train and sharpen your saw through education. Whether it's in-person training/conferences, virtual, or online, there are usually numerous quality opportunities for leadership training specific to our professions, and applicable to leadership in general. As you plan out your calendar for the next few months or year, include training. I personally like to attend some in-person trainings when I know there are going to be networking opportunities. The more relationships we build with other leaders, the more expansive our resource pool becomes.

Copious amounts of research on leadership demonstrates a direct correlation between the effectiveness of leaders and their participation in leadership development and training. Leadership training does equate to a positive outcome on individual performance, it also better equips them to influence employee performance and effectiveness.[47] The Institute of Management Development (IMD) described the opportunities provided to people in recognized leadership positions by stating the following:

Leadership skills training programs typically offer multiple benefits. Finding the right training program can help you build the skills necessary to advance your career. Leadership skills training encourages managers and leaders to:

- Find new, innovative ways of developing and managing people.
- Challenge themselves and identify who they want to be as a leader.

---

[47] "Why and When Leadership Training Predicts Effectiveness . . . - Researchgate." Accessed March 16, 2023.
https://www.researchgate.net/publication/324620698_Why_and_when_leadership_training_predicts_effectiveness_The_role_of_leader_identity_and_leadership_experience.

- Tackle the broader societal issues they face and how leaders contribute to that.
- Develop the emotional intelligence to handle different situations.[48]

IMD stated that training and education can enhance a leader's ability to develop people, identify who they are (purpose as a leader) and utilize emotional intelligence in their leadership role.

Now, I have survived numerous, boring leadership classes . . . I mean instructor reading the PowerPoint word for word in a deathly monotone voice kind of training. There is nothing worse. Most of those classes I attended were required for me to be eligible for promotion or receive certain "supervisor" certifications. I am now much more selective about the training I choose. If the leadership training you have participated in was boring, try to select something else more engaging and informative. I get it . . . we all have some training that is required for our jobs that we have no choice but to attend. Unfortunately, some of the worst leadership trainers are our bosses! Take the time to explore other more innovative and interesting classes to attend or participate in virtually. Referring to IMD again, they provided the following four considerations regarding how to determine if an educational entity will afford you top notch, innovative training:

1) A proven track record of success.
2) Offers both standard and customized training programs.
3) Sees training as a process, not an isolated event.
4) Measures effectiveness and impact.

It's important to make sure you are exposing yourself as much as possible to other successful leaders. Beyond reading, there are

[48] "The 8 Key Benefits of a Leadership Skills Training in 2023." IMD business school for management and leadership courses, January 27, 2023. https://www.imd.org/reflections/leadership-skills-training-program/.

numerous avenues for learning from quality leaders. Podcasts, TED Talks and YouTube Channels are just a few examples of informative and entertaining tools that can be utilized for your growth. Remember what I said about stories? I learn more from leaders who share stories that connect to the leadership principles they have been successful in implementing. Research what's out there. Get recommendations from people you trust not to lead you into a training wasteland, but instead, something you will actually find beneficial.

Let me add one more potential education tool for you to consider . . . furthering your education. I am aware that school is not for everyone. I don't believe that you have to have a certain degree to be successful in leadership. However, I have gained so much insight into numerous topics that have led me to be a more well-rounded leader through academic education. There are several factors that must be examined when considering whether or not to attend college or strive to obtain a graduate degree. Finances, family dynamics, workload, and schedule are all elements that will determine the viability of going back to school. Online degrees are more widely available than ever. Although I don't love that learning style, the reading and research I did for my graduate degrees were extremely beneficial. If you can figure out a way to make it happen, I highly suggest you look into it. Some of you may be intimidated (or terrified) at the thought of going back to school. I have been there. When I was considering getting my doctorate, one of my greatest fears was having to take the GRE. I had not looked at a geometry problem (I really hated geometry) since my sophomore year in high school. Yet, I went into full GRE prep mode and made it happen. I promise you, if I can do it, you can as well.

EVALUATION

A part of your job is evaluating others. Are they meeting the goals and standards that have been set? Are they meeting the mission? Are they productive and proactive? Many of us have to do quarterly or annual evaluations of our employees. The question is, who is evaluating us? Maybe you have a boss that evaluates you. Beyond our bosses possibly helping us see where we need to grow, we don't get a lot of feedback on how we are doing because, well, our people are not going to naturally come knock on our door and tell us where we need to improve. However, one of the ways we grow and remain sharp is by discovering where we are lacking.

Therefore, we need to become intentional in seeking out the evaluation of others. If you have a person you directly report to, that is a good place to start. If they are not giving you constructive feedback, go ask for it. The person I now report to is new to the job. The first time we had lunch together, I asked him to please provide constructive feedback, especially when I am not meeting his expectations. Beyond that, all the people who report directly to me on our leadership staff have been asked on more than one occasion to let me know where I am struggling or flat out failing as a leader. It took a while, but I think they would all tell you now that I am very much open to their feedback because I know they are giving it to me for my own good.

EMULATION

You were challenged to demonstrate effective, compelling force leadership for those you have the privilege of leading. In order to keep yourself sharp, you need some leaders in your life that emulate the kind of leader you are striving to be. When I first became a chief, I was very intentional in meeting with some experienced chiefs that were the kind of leaders I knew I wanted to emulate. Some of the ideas I have shared in this book came from them. When I come across personnel issues not exactly covered in the "Leadership 101" book, I won't hesitate to call and ask for some guidance. As I shared before, when my passion tank is running a little low, the group I meet with monthly provides a much needed refueling of my passion. When I attend conferences, I often grow from simply connecting and networking with other leaders.

Also, the books I read (last time on reading . . . I promise) are often from leaders that emulate transformational leadership. When I listen to podcasts, I typically listen to leaders who model what I am striving to be as a leader. When I go to conferences, I try to go to classes that are being taught by people who demonstrate what's important when it comes to influencing others. There are people on our leadership team that mirror what compelling force leadership looks like. That's another advantage of promoting the right people to help lead your team. For the most part, I am very intentional in surrounding myself with like-minded leaders. Nonetheless, don't be afraid to connect with leaders that are different than you. You would be surprised at some of the insight you might gain from those who see leadership from a different perspective. Ultimately, surround yourself with men and women who lead people with purpose and passion. One of the most effective ways to keep your saw sharp is by staying connected with sharp leaders.

PRACTICAL POINTS

Like every other area of leading yourself, you have to be intentional in ensuring you continue to grow and develop. This won't happen by accident. Your schedule and your budget need to demonstrate a commitment to never stop growing as a leader. Some practical ideas:

Avoid the Status Quo

A question I often ask our staff, and myself, when making operational decisions, or when we are analyzing where we need to improve is . . . If we were starting a brand-new department tomorrow, with an endless budget and no other constraints to limit our imagination, what would that look like? Just today, I had a meeting with some of our leaders about our training department. This question was asked, and I loved some of the responses I heard. Is it plausible or affordable? Maybe, maybe not. But man, I loved the ideas shared that can help us work toward being more innovative and effective in our training department. Do we have budgets and other constraints that are sometimes roadblocks to bigger and better things? Yes. However, we need to get in the habit of thinking about how to get bigger and better and stop practicing a type of thinking that diminishes growth and innovation.

Education

Ideally, you can grow and develop with education and training that is specific to your profession. But don't be afraid to go outside of your profession for development opportunities. Some of the best leadership training I have attended was led by people who had absolutely no connection to Public Safety. Yet, so many of the leadership ideas shared correlate to any leadership role, regardless of the profession. Also, I have garnered amazing ideas from these types of training opportunities . . . ideas that are typically unheard of in our profession. These are the kind of concepts that can ignite innovative and successful strategies that can lead us to engaging in new and exciting initiatives.

There are several successful corporations that actually have leadership roles dedicated to overseeing organizational culture and employee growth. I can assure you, that is not the norm in my line of work, yet we are attempting to try our own version of this approach. We are realigning some leadership roles to allow more focus on culture-related initiatives. Granted, these roles will still entail many of the traditional command-level responsibilities, but with an additional emphasis on creating an environment where people are more apt to desire to be an engaged team member. Will it work? I'll have to get back to you on that one, but I am very optimistic.

Evaluation

One of the most effective, and somewhat painful evaluations I utilized was a 360 evaluation assessment. This was given to my direct reports, line-level leaders, peers (other department directors), and my supervisor. There were some areas of weakness I was not surprised to see, but there were other areas I did not see coming. Once I got over the initial sting, I looked at the results as an opportunity to grow and get better. I used a local leadership development company to come in and do the evaluation. There are also several resources you can find online that can help provide you with the tools you need to make this happen.

Also, another great source of seeing areas of improvement for yourself is through the surveys I discussed earlier. As you get honest feedback on the good and bad of your team, division, or organization, you will likely become aware of some areas for you to improve on as a leader. There will be some obvious connections between what is not going well and what you should be doing to address it. Again, a growth opportunity.

Emulation

Networking is paramount. If opportunities to connect with other leaders is not happening, take the initiative to step up and create some ongoing, scheduled gatherings with leaders in your area. If geography is an issue regarding getting together in person, the virtual environment creates numerous options to connect with other leaders, regardless of where they are located. Maybe there are already some existing groups that could help sharpen your saw. Be intentional about connecting with those groups or even creating one.

If you have a couple of local leaders that provide you an example of what you are striving for as a leader, call them up and offer to take them to lunch to benefit from their experience and expertise. If they are compelling force, influential leaders, they will be more than happy to help another leader looking for some guidance and mentoring.

" Don't ever lose sight of the fact that serving in leadership is a privilege. **"**

Chapter 14

CONCLUSION

I HAVE A love-hate relationship with roller coasters. I love going fast, and I love the thrill and adventure of twists, turns, riding upside down and other surprises that come along with a well-designed roller coaster. What I hate is how sick I get when I ride one. I absolutely detest being nauseated. I would rather be in excruciating pain than suffer from nausea, which is exactly what happens when I ride a roller coaster. Apparently, the older you get, the worse motion sickness becomes. A few years ago, I tried one of the virtual rides at a Universal park . . . you know, the kind that doesn't really move, and you literally just sit there and watch a screen. Yep . . . same result. Sick as a dog. In my defense, I did learn after some random episodes of severe dizziness that started occurring while I was sitting still that I have a pretty significant case of vertigo. So, there's my excuse.

I grew up going to Six Flags. It was approximately fifteen minutes from where I lived, and I got a season pass every year. I actually worked there for a summer. So, it was kind of cool to eventually take my own kids to the same park I grew up attending. However, my last visit to Six Flags with the kids wasn't so cool. My youngest daughter was still pretty young at the time, and as we were finishing up our day, she decided she wanted to ride the newest roller coaster, Goliath. She wanted me to be the one that rode with her. As you can imagine, I wasn't overly excited about this because of my issues with roller coasters and nausea. There was also a two-hour wait to ride, which removed any remaining enthusiasm I might have had about experiencing Goliath. In my mind, there is no ride on the face of the planet good enough to wait two hours to ride. But she was a daddy's girl and, well . . . enough said. My wife and the other kids went and rode other rides, and we got in line.

As we finally got close to getting on, she suddenly started having second thoughts and wanted to back out . . . *after* waiting in line for almost two hours. That's right, two hours. I, of course, was committed at this point—we were going to ride Goliath, come hell or high water. So, we got on, and we began the climb. The first hill was extremely high, and she was screaming and crying all the way to the top. Once we got over that first hill and really got moving, her fear converted into joy. She was having a blast! And so was I . . . for about a minute. The thrill of moving at a high rate of speed while maneuvering twists and turns was awesome—until it wasn't. About halfway through the ride, I got extremely sick. By the time we got off, I could hardly walk. You would have thought I had just finished off a long night of hard drinking. I would have miserably failed a field sobriety test. My wonderful wife drove us all home. As soon as we arrived, I headed straight for the bathroom. I remained there for the rest of the evening alternating between lying on the floor and getting up just long enough to throw up, and then lying back down on the floor again.

You hopefully have enjoyed the thrill of the ride of leadership at times in your career. Adding value to people by leading with purpose and passion can be an awesome and fulfilling experience. Conversely, you have also probably had those moments where you felt disoriented and down for the count, as I did on my bathroom floor. Even when you do things well, those moments will inevitably come. The key is to try to remember why we do what we do. I can assure you, riding Goliath would have never crossed my mind if it had just been me. Part of the misery of standing in line for two hours was feeling fairly confident I was waiting a long time to do something that would result in making me miserable, which it did.

But I didn't ride it for me. I rode it for my daughter. The wait and the ride were all about her. The same goes for leading. When things are good, it's not about you and me. And, when we have those moments when we are flat on our faces, it is still not about you and me. It's about the people we have the privilege of leading. Our people should always be a part of our why . . . our purpose. A compelling force leader who emphasizes people, purpose, and passion is the kind of leader that is in the game for the long haul. There has been a lot of good stuff written on the keys to effective leadership. I could talk for hours about other important topics like leadership theories, strategic approaches to productivity, generational differences in employees, the importance of emotional intelligence, etc. There are numerous specific books written on each of those topics. You should read as many as possible. Yet, I am convinced that putting your people ahead of yourself is where true leadership success always begins. Of all the things I have learned about this topic, I can honestly say that if you make what you do about your people, and treat them well, you can figure out most everything else. Is there a need for a certain level of competence? Of course. Is hard work required? No doubt. Do you need to be purpose-driven? We have definitely established you do. Nevertheless, if everything you do centers on adding value to your people, your chances for true success as a leader is greatly enhanced, and you can learn the other stuff along the way.

Don't ever lose sight of the fact that serving in leadership is a privilege. With the correct mindset and approach, you have the opportunity to add value to others through your influence. Think about the coaches you have played for . . . the teachers that you studied under . . . the leaders you have worked for that had a significant impact on you. Those are people in your life you will never forget. You can have the same effect on those you have the opportunity to serve as a compelling force leader. Your impact will especially be prevalent if you lead with purpose and passion. One characteristic my favorite coaches, teachers, and leaders shared was a love for their jobs and a love for those they led and influenced. Someone you have influenced may share the same sentiment about you one day.

Leaders are coaches, and coaches are leaders. As the coach of your team, you need a game plan. Some game plans are more elaborate than others. Your playbook at work may need to be very detailed and specific. Job descriptions, sales goals, growth projections, project management, player development, customer acquisition, etc., may all be part of your winning strategy. What I hope you have discovered, or been reminded of, in this book is regardless of what kind of work you do, the winning game plan for all leaders is to center your playbook around your people, while being purpose-driven and utilizing your passion to stay effective and inspire your team toward bigger and better things.

I will often ask some of the compelling force leaders (both ranked and unranked) in our agency to meet me at my favorite coffee spot. We will talk family, sports, and whatever other random topics come up organically. Regardless, we always end up discussing leadership. It's a chance for me to hear from them and get their perspective on what's happening with our team, good or bad. It's also an opportunity for me to dig a little deeper into their view of leadership and hopefully encourage them and maybe even help them in their leadership journey. Ultimately, we talk leadership over coffee, in a very comfortable environment.

I hope as you have read this book, it at times felt like we were having a conversation over coffee. My goal in writing this was to provide whatever it is you need to be a compelling force leader. There is a chance you already know the advantages of transformational leadership, and this provided you with some confirmation that your approach is on target. You may disagree with some or most of what I have said. But if that makes you step back and analyze your approach to leadership, that's a good thing. Or maybe you are new to the leadership game, and you need some help developing a game plan for the future. The 3P Leadership approach is a great place to start. Regardless, I am grateful you took the time to read this. I sincerely appreciate it. This has been a true joy for me. If you ever find yourself in the Atlanta area and want to talk leadership, reach out to me. I know a great spot where we can meet.

ACKNOWLEDGMENTS

SPECIAL THANKS TO Pastor Mike Linch, Brian Will, and Michael Warren. When I had the idea to write a book, I sent you all a very rough draft of my first few chapters because I respect you and your input. Your feedback and support was very helpful and inspired me to move forward with this crazy idea.

Thank you, Steve Beecham, for spending time with me talking about the process of writing a book. Also, thank you for pointing me in the right direction regarding finding a publisher.

BookLogix, you made writing a book a much more seamless process than I ever imagined. I am grateful for your honest feedback and expertise as it relates to writing and publishing books.

Finally, a very special thanks to my wonderful wife, Lori. Once again, I came to you with a crazy, time-consuming idea, and once again you backed me 100 percent. Life is better because of you, and I am better because of you. I love you.

ABOUT THE AUTHOR

DR. JOHN ROBISON has over fifteen years of leadership experience in the public safety profession, and he currently serves as Director of Public Safety, where he leads over 250 police officers, firefighters, and 911 dispatchers. Before that, he served as police chief of a metro Atlanta agency. John is also a leadership instructor for a national training agency where he teaches and develops leaders from organizations throughout the country. Additionally, John works as an instructor for two different universities in Georgia. Most importantly, John is blessed to be married to his wonderful wife, Lori, and a father to amazing adult children.